CAREERS IN ELECTIVE GOVERNMENT

This is a comprehensive look at the various careers open to young people in the vital area of elective government. Through the means of personal interviews, the author has compiled a vast amount of material to aid the young person in the quest for job opportunity and fulfillment. He tells teenagers how they can start becoming a part of the government—either by actually running for office, or by getting introduced to local officials and volunteering for jobs, or through intern programs. Chapters include women in government, campaigning, lobbyists, ethics in government. Numerous employees discuss job positions such as the legislative researcher, the executive secretary, the general staff member, the legislative counsel, and the legislative analyst, to name just a few. An important feature of the book is the section at the end of each chapter suggesting specific activities the young person can do *now* in the pursuit of a career in elective government.

BOOKS BY ROBERT V. DOYLE

CAREERS IN ELECTIVE GOVERNMENT
YOUR CAREER IN INTERIOR DESIGN

Careers in
Elective
Government

ROBERT V. DOYLE

with photographs

Julian Messner
New York

Published by Julian Messner, a Division of Simon & Schuster, Inc.
1 West 39 Street, New York, N. Y. 10018. All rights reserved.

To Twig, Bobby, and Wendy, with love

Library of Congress Cataloging in Publication Data

Doyle, Robert V
  Careers in elective government.

  Bibliography: p. 205
  Includes index.
  1. Civil service positions—United States. I. Title.
JK716.D68   353′.00023   75-46500
ISBN 0-671-32790-9
ISBN 0-671-32791-7 lib. bdg.

Printed in the United States of America

CONTENTS

A WORD FROM
THE AUTHOR

This journey through the exciting sphere of elective government was impelled partly out of necessity and partly out of intellectual curiosity. Certain writing assignments for national periodicals pointed out personal areas of ignorance concerning our concepts of the "inner workings" of elective government.

As we delved into our research, we sought answers to more and more questions that bloomed with the profusion of a well-tended fruit tree. The more we picked and pruned, cultivated and fed the project, the larger, more important it became.

We began *Careers in Elective Government* without sextant or compass or road map, exactly as the students of Rio Bueno High School may have in Chapter 1.

But on our voyage we received so much assistance from those wonderful American citizens with whom we came in contact, that not to name them would be tantamount to snubbing a good friend—for that is what each has become.

Helen Graper, Don Dellmann, and Jeff Serdahely, all from Wisconsin; Jeff's brother, Doug, from Alaska; and Doug's law partner, Shelley Higgins. Shelley's ex-roommate, Susan Sawyer, now in the California state capitol; Doug's ex-roommate, Stewart (Sandy) Kemp, in Cambridge (perhaps back in Washington, D.C. by now).

Virginia Howery, from D.C., who offered encouragement and opened doors.

The former assistant to the president of the United States, Secretary of Defense Donald Rumsfeld, who helped make the White House come to life in these pages. United States senators Alan Cranston (California) and Mike Gravel (Alaska); members of the House of Representatives, Bella Abzug, New York, and Barry Goldwater, Jr., California; California Assemblyman Robert P. Nimmo and California state Senator Clare Berryhill; the mayors: John Ray Harrison of the city of Pasadena, Texas; Richard H. Marriott, of Sacramento, California; and Harry J. Parrish, Manassas, Virginia. Each of these elected officials was nonpolitically gracious in his help.

The staff: Dorothy O'Brien, Washington, D.C., executive secretary to California Representative Robert Leggett; Leggett's Sacramento field secretary Virginia Harper, and administrative assistant/case worker Ed Meeker; Jackie Habecker, receptionist par excellence for five California governors; Cecilia Ward, innovative, efficient secretary in the California Assembly. All these people were extraordinary in offering their valuable assistance.

To Vivian Miksak, coordinator of the California Assembly Internship Program, we owe a special "thank you" for taking time from a busy schedule to introduce us to the burgeoning national internship/fellowship activities in which her expertise has been beneficial. We also wish to remember James R. McCauley, coordinator for the new California Senate Internship Program, for his assistance and advice to students seeking experience and involvement through internships.

It was a distinct pleasure working with Dr. Sharlene Pearlman Hirsch, National Director of Executive High School Internships of America; her Sacramento coordinator, Ms. Sandra Verlinde; and all the cheerfully competent students we met through the High School Internship program.

Heald's Business College vice-president Kathryn Leles, and members of her staff and faculty, including Edna B. Groves and Elta Langbehn, were extremely helpful in the secretarial preparation and placement field.

Our thanks also to professional campaign consultants and convention managers, including Joe Cerrell, Harvey Englander, Mardi Gregory, Terri Jones, Dick Rosengarten, and Ann Blumlein, to name but a few; younger activists such as Dwayne Adams and Paul Cheverton; the selfless young lobbyists as exemplified by Judi Phillips. All of these individuals conducted us through a world of excitement about which we had read a little, but had never realized the extent to which so many hard-working Americans are involved.

We wish to thank all the librarians who were so patient with us during our research, particularly Chloris Noblet of the Sacramento City Central Library, who not only helped us find our way through a maze of research material, but was optimistically supportive throughout.

The value of Hank Parkinson's *Campaign Insight*, and his generosity in making this periodical available to us, has no limits.

Also, we appreciate the editorial balance and insight provided by Iris D. Rosoff of Julian Messner.

And let's not forget Margie, who has remained steadfast through earthquakes, record-high weather extremes, late-night-hours of typing, and the strange sleeping and eating habits and daytime moods on the part of the author, to whom she has been married long enough to become not only tolerant—but lovingly understanding.

To all of you: my humble thanks.

Mothers all want their sons to grow up to be President, but they don't want them to become politicians in the process.

John F. Kennedy

PREFACE

The genius of republican liberty seems to demand . . . that all power should be derived from the people, but that those intrusted with it should be kept in dependence on the people, by a short duration of their appointments; and that even during this short period the trust should be placed not in a few, but a number of hands.

James Madison
"The Federalist Papers"
Number 37–1787

Our objectives today are the same as those of Madison's (and Hamilton's) constitutional government. We seek an orderly, fair, and economically practical manner in which to carry on the business of government.

To reach these ends, people are needed.

Not an elite. Just a generous supply of extraordinary citizens.

People who want to serve.

People who are willing to commit themselves to learning the ramifications of elective government, and dedicate themselves for "a short duration," to become "intrusted with" the power from the people.

In short, people for people, as officials or as staff.

We, in the beginning of our tercentenary, act from a series of elective, interlocked, tax-supported stages: city, county, state, national; school boards, tax boards, boards of public utilities; legislative, judicial, and executive.

Recent and current history point out with unmistakable clarity and urgency the need for trustworthy Americans in all city, state, and federal elective offices.

For the purpose of inspiring people—particularly the young, newly enfranchised citizens of the United States—to become involved in the public sector and to seek careers in elective government, this book has been written.

The term "elective government" has been carefully chosen. The government of civil service bureaucracy—working for the state—is dull compared with elective government, where the policy makers and the action are. Yet often one may find the way into the "exempt group" through bureaucratic channels.

In the civil service exempt status of elective government, the power—and job security—is dependent on the people, exemplified through the voting booth. In the bureaucracy, the strength is contained in civil service laws.

Elective government needs the bureaucracy to administer its dictums; the bureaucracy functions through many shifts of power as time or voter dissatisfaction limits terms in office.

As Madison wrote:

A frequent change of men will result from a frequent return of elections; and a frequent change of measures from a frequent change of men; . . .

It is this "frequent change" that makes elective government an interesting amalgam. Not only do individual offices see different occupants through varied courses of time, but the office holders themselves often see many job changes throughout their careers.

In the climate of frequent change thrive countless exciting, lucrative career opportunities, many of which we will outline on the following pages.

We have assumed that you are a serious student with, at least to a small degree, some political leanings. You are willing to plan for your future and have the desire to strive for excellence.

Through an apochryphal device we will take you from a classroom in a fictitious city, Rio Bueno, into the very real world of American politics. Through the statements of office holders and staff assistants, past and present, we will introduce you to political life.

With the help of those who have been there, we will show you how to start your long-range program leading to elective government, give you a list of educational steps to take, and point you down a hallway with many doors.

We will delineate opportunities in local government to "get your feet wet." We will offer a passport into your state capitol; we will hand you a figurative ticket to Washington, D.C.

We will take you to a pair of party conventions, and introduce you to the people who run them.

You will want to know about the staff jobs available to you, and understand the important chores with which the staff contends.

You will learn about the legislative researcher and the multifaceted job of the executive secretary, the administrative assistant and the necessity for counsel.

There are also many opportunities open to those who qualify as interns, in the legislature and in other areas of government. We will give you detailed information on internships and fellowships.

You will find two words repeated throughout our study: *involve* and *volunteer*. When you first become involved with elective government, it will undoubtedly be as a volunteer.

If you volunteer to work for an election campaign committee, you will be able to refer to our stories of factual experiences on how elections have been won through honest effort, much of it done by volunteers, who were all involved activists.

Should campaigning appeal to you, we offer information on the many full-time job opportunities in campaign management.

Of course, you may aspire to public office right now!

We will tell you about successful candidates, many of them in their teens and twenties, and we will give you tips on how to win elections.

Two adjuncts to elective government that offer career choices are the legislative advocate (lobbyist) and the legislative analyst. Each is a good field for steady employment.

Finally, we offer information to the average voter who may never become actively involved in elective government, but would like to add to a personal reservoir of knowledge.

We believe politics to be an honorable profession.

It needs you—now more than ever.

Robert V. Doyle, 1976

ACKNOWLEDGMENTS

For permission to excerpt and reprint copyrighted material in this book, the author and publisher are grateful to the following:

Atheneum Publishers
for excerpts from POLITICAL OBLIGATION by Richard E. Flathman. Copyright © 1972 by Richard E. Flathman.
American Political Science Association
for excerpts from an article "The Record of Congress in Committee Staffing" by Gladys M. Kammerer. *American Political Science Association Review*, No. 4, December 1951.
Basic Books, Inc.
for excerpts from POLITICAL WOMAN by Jeanne J. Kirkpatrick. Copyright © 1974 by Center for the American Woman and Politics.
British Broadcasting Corporation
for excerpt from "The Ascent of Man" (television series) by Dr. Jacob Bronowski. "BBC copyright."
Crown Publishers, Inc.
for excerpts from THE SECRET BOSS OF CALIFORNIA by Arthur H. Samish and Bob Thomas. Copyright © 1971 by Arthur H. Samish and Robert Thomas.

The John Day Co.
for excerpt from THE FUTURE OF INDUSTRIAL MAN by Peter F. Drucker. Copyright © 1942 (renewed 1970) by Peter F. Drucker.

Doubleday and Company
for excerpt from O CONGRESS by Donald Riegle with Trevor Armbrister. Copyright © 1972 by Donald W. Riegle, Jr. and Trevor Armbrister.

Harper's Weekly
for excerpts from an article "Why We're a Nation of Illiterates" by Joan Geier, *Harper's Weekly,* June 6, 1975. Copyright © 1975 by *Harper's Weekly.* Reprinted by special permission.

Harper & Row, Publishers, Inc.
for excerpts from HIGH ON FOGGY BOTTOM by Charles Frankel, Harper & Row, 1969.

International City Management Association
for excerpts from International City Management Association, THE MUNICIPAL YEAR BOOK 1974. "Inside the Year Book." (Washington, D.C., International City Management Association, 1974).

Little, Brown and Company
for excerpt from THE EPIC OF AMERICA by James Truslow Adams. Copyright © 1931, 1932 by James Truslow Adams. Copyright © renewed 1959 by Mrs. James Truslow Adams. Reprinted by permission of Little, Brown and Co. in association with The Atlantic Monthly Press.

Frank Logue
for excerpts from *Who Administers?* Published by The Ford Foundation.

McGraw-Hill Book Company
for excerpt from OBSTACLE COURSE ON CAPITOL HILL by Robert Bendiner. Copyright © 1964 by Robert Bendiner.

The National Center for Public Service Internship Programs
for excerpts from A DIRECTORY OF PUBLIC SERVICE INTERNSHIPS by Richard Ungerer, 1974-75.

Walker & Company
for excerpt from UNDERSTANDING OUR CONSTITUTION by
Jethro K. Lieberman. Copyright © 1967 by Jethro K.
Lieberman.

Connecticut Walker
for excerpts from his article "Young Men at the Top in
Washington" published in *Parade* magazine, June 1, 1975.

John Wiley and Sons
for excerpts from WOMEN IN POLITICS, edited by Jane S.
Jaquette. Copyright © 1974 by John Wiley and Sons, Inc.

Writer's Digest
for excerpts from an article "References and Resources"
published in *Writer's Digest*, June 1975. Copyright © 1975
by *Writer's Digest*.

Chapter

1. THE BEGINNING OF A PROJECT

The smells of early spring floated through Mr. Corcoran's classroom windows.

He debated with himself about closing them to keep out the raucous sounds of the baseball squad in after-school practice. The Student Council members would arrive within minutes, and he wanted to hold their attention without distraction. Spring fever was a most difficult opponent, and this meeting was important.

He wiped the blackboard clean and wrote in large letters:

Subject of today's meeting:
CAREER DAY!!!

Putting down the chalk, he walked slowly toward the window. He stretched his arms and scratched his curly beard. A youngish man of medium build, at times he seemed hardly older than some of the more mature boys in his classes. Admittedly, he had spring fever too. He paused for a moment, reached for the window-pole, and then let his hand fall to his side.

It was too nice a day to close it out.

The clatter of feet in the hallway, the giggle of girls' voices, and a boy's laugh told the teacher that the Student Council had arrived.

Mr. Corcoran smiled at them as they straggled in, called each by name, and waved them up toward the front of the room.

There were eighteen students in all: presidents, vice-presidents, secretaries, and treasurers of the tenth, eleventh, and twelfth grades; four student body officers; the Yell Leader; and a reporter from the Rio Bueno High School *Foursquare*.

"Some of you have been through this before," Mr. Corcoran began, sitting casually on the front edge of his scarred oak desk. "Those of you who have been in on a previous Career Day planning session, please help expedite the meeting. It's too nice to stay inside, and the quicker we get down to business, the sooner we will be finished."

Nancy, the senior class secretary, always the joker, made a move for the door. "Let's go," she said, pretending to leave.

Mr. Corcoran, accustomed to minor disturbances, pushed ahead with his subject.

"As you know, we have had Career Days at Rio Bueno High for the past seven years, and, according to our records, many graduating students have found it a valuable experience. Follow-up questionnaires to former students have shown that Career Day helped many of them decide on their immediate employment choices and longer term goals. So we know it's worthwhile. But we have a problem. We must decide on sixty careers from a choice of about eighty, because we have limited time and facilities. There is also a problem in getting speakers for some areas of employment. What we have to do here today is line up sixty careers with some assurance that we will have speakers to fill the spots. You are here as representatives of the student body. You have had a week to talk it up on campus, and to ask questions and get the thinking of the students. So let's get busy and make the list."

Turning the meeting over to Chuck, football tackle and

student body president, Mr. Corcoran took a seat in the fourth row and watched with pleasure the smooth manner in which the husky athlete handled the procedure.

With Jean, the student body secretary, listing careers on the blackboard, each officer took a turn introducing vocations. Mr. Corcoran watched quietly as each individual made proposals. As the list grew longer, he found himself enjoying this part of his own career: observing the rare blossoms of a new generation unfold. Each student had his or her own personality, drive, and ambition. None of this group lacked these attributes. A good sense of humor prevailed. All were voluble, eager to get into the act.

Except Philip, the sophomore president.

Selected by the tenth graders in a rather underkeyed, orderly election last October, Philip was as quiet as the others were loud. He seemed to be pacing himself, waiting silently for his chance to be heard. Not a big boy, really. Slender. Wiry. Dark hair, very dark brown eyes. Quiet, yes, but he had something—an air of self-assurance that made him noticeable when he wished it. Like now. He was standing, asking for the floor.

"I think we should have a speaker on politics," he said, standing sideways at his place on the far aisle to face the others.

"Politics," someone groaned.

"My dad says all politicians are crooks," offered Steve, glancing at Gladys who nodded in assent.

"Politics is so dead," Wendy cried out. "Who'd want to get into that?"

Philip stood quietly, waiting for the furor to subside.

"Anyway, who'd take the time to come and talk to us, even if we could get thirty-five sign-ups for the hour?" The Yell Leader was Artimus, now standing, speaking. "Those guys don't have much time for us high schoolers."

A good thought, Mr. Corcoran mused. The Council that

sat regularly in the Rio Bueno City Hall seldom visited the high school, although at least two of the members had children enrolled as students.

As the debate rose to a din, Chuck hammered on the desk with the flat side of a book. "Hold it a minute," he said, his voice charged with authority. "We were told to cut the number of speakers and subjects from eighty to sixty. We've never had politics as a subject before, and if we can't find room for everyone now, I don't see how we can add a new subject."

"I thought there might be a problem," Philip answered, stepping forward, a paper in his hand. "I knew that there had never been anyone from government to speak on Career Day before. But I talked to a few of my friends in the tenth grade, and we came up with the idea that it might make a good program. So I started a petition, and I have thirty names of students who would like to hear what politics is all about."

He laid the paper on the desk in front of the president and returned to his place, but remained standing.

"Oh, wow," said Artimus, smiling broadly now. "You sure know how to do it."

He surely does, Mr. Corcoran agreed silently. But where would the speaker come from? It was easy enough to get people from the airlines, or the plumbers' union, or electrical engineers, people who worked on salaries and would be paid for their time by their employers. In addition, certain professional people—doctors, dentists, lawyers—were willing to give up a few hours a year to consult with young students. But more often than not, Mr. Corcoran thought with some sadness, it was difficult to fill a program with speakers.

Philip, however, wasn't through.

"As for a speaker," he was saying, "Mayor Martinez has already told me that he would be happy to talk with a group, if they would be really interested in hearing him."

Mr. Corcoran suppressed a grin with some effort.

Chuck turned to look at the blackboard. Over forty careers were listed in neat columns. He knew that at least a dozen or more popular subjects were still to be named. Yet Philip had his petition. Turning back to the assembled school officers, he asked, "Shall we add politics?"

Cathy, the junior class president, called out, "I move we include politics as a career."

"It isn't necessary to make a motion, Cathy. Just show me hands. . . ."

Hands shot up around the room—a clear majority.

"Okay, let's have Mayor Martinez," Chuck said.

Jean wrote politics at the top of a new column.

"Philip," Chuck continued, "you clear it with the mayor, and tell him we'll send a letter of confirmation next week."

Then he clapped his hands together smartly. "All right," he proclaimed. "We're going good now. Let's finish the list and get out the invitations tomorrow."

By two o'clock on Career Day, the students of Rio Bueno High School had heard experts from many fields discuss their occupations: firemen and police (including a petite woman sergeant); soldiers, sailors, flyers, and mechanics from the Armed Services; secretaries, chefs, and interior designers. Over all, the full quota of sixty professions and trades was represented.

Each student had been given a choice of five potential means of livelihood, the mysteries of which—if not completely solved—were at least explored. Now, coming down to the day's last scheduled period, the students were almost satiated with the knowledge they had consumed.

In Mr. Corcoran's room, selected by the Student Council for the lone political presentation, an overflow crowd had assembled, taking every desk and available chair, and lining the side and back walls.

Just as the five-after bell sounded, with students pushing into corners and general confusion reigning, Mayor Martinez made his entrance.

The entrance was heralded by a television cameraman backing into the room. An aide carrying a bright floodlight stepped nimbly around, keeping the light on the mayor's face as he strode quickly through the door.

Manuel Martinez was a short, stocky man, with a receding rim of black hair and bushy curls partially covering his ears.

Beside the mayor was a young dark-haired woman, smiling brightly and carrying a briefcase. Behind them a tall, young man, modishly dressed, also smiling in friendly fashion, followed.

The entourage, guided by Philip, came to the front of the classroom, and the students stood and clapped, taking Philip's lead. The mayor was obviously enjoying the occasion— the tumult and excitement his presence produced pleased him. Suddenly, however, he waved his hand. The bright floodlight was extinguished after a final panning of the room, and the mayor began to speak.

"Okay, fellows," he told the television men, "that's it for now. I'll be available for a statement later, but right now I've got some important people to talk to," he gestured toward the assembled students, "off the record."

The two television people hurried from the room as the mayor began to speak without any introduction. Mr. Corcoran was not familiar with the guest; he only knew him from the election items that appeared in the newspapers and on the television.

"Philip Alvarez has told me that there are some things you want to know about politics. Right?" the mayor began.

Not waiting for an answer, he turned to Philip, who had taken his seat in the front row. "Well, Philip, here I am."

Philip reddened slightly, and shifted self-consciously in his seat.

"Well, there's one thing you have to get used to in politics, if you're even a little successful," the mayor continued. "You've got to get used to being followed around by television cameramen." The students smiled, not sure whether they should laugh. "Since the FCC ruling, television is really hungry for local news. And since the voters have changed our system from a weak-mayor/council concept to a strong-mayor/council system, which makes my position much more vulnerable, it seems those two go everywhere with me—except into my home."

The mayor hit his forehead and rolled his eyes, and this time the students laughed, feeling at ease with their visitor.

The mayor leaned easily on the front edge of Mr. Corcoran's desk. He was dressed in a dark blue business suit, a pale blue shirt, and a brightly colored print bow-tie.

"First I want you to meet some nice people," he said to the students, turning to his two aides who were seated in straight-backed chairs behind the desk. "Mary Lucas, my executive secretary."

Mary smiled and nodded pleasantly.

"And my administrative assistant, Mr. Donald Dixon." Dixon smiled too, waving casually toward the assembly.

Martinez told a few fast one-line jokes in which he was the fall guy, pointing up the need for able assistants in a mayor's office.

"Now, I want to tell you some things about government," the mayor said after he sensed that his listeners were on his side. "I want to tell you how it is, how they say it is, how it isn't, and how it should be. That's a big order for . . . what do I have? . . . forty-five minutes? Well, we can get a good start in forty-five minutes, but I've been in politics for fifteen of my thirty-seven years, so it will take some editing to tell it all."

He became serious, folding his arms across his chest, standing straddle-legged before the group.

"You want to know who I really am?" He hesitated. "I'm your servant. I know it sounds corny. But I have been hired to administer the city offices and stand guardian over the city tax moneys and lead the City Council. I've been hired through the ballot, and any time I don't do the job I've been hired to do, I can be fired through the ballot. Then I'd be just Manny Martinez, and I would go back to the clothing business with my father and brothers."

Pausing, he surveyed the faces looking up at him. All the students were very quiet now, listening carefully to his words.

"All that business of having the TV guys take my picture coming in here—do you know how much they'd want to take my picture for tonight's news if I weren't mayor?" He snapped his fingers. "That much. Nothing."

Mr. Corcoran, standing in the rear of the crowded room, watched with interest as the mayor warmed to his subject.

Pointing a forefinger straight out, Mayor Martinez swiftly changed his stance, leaning toward the students now.

"But that's the challenge of elective government," he said forcefully. "To earn your job. Then to hang on to it while everyone is trying to take it away from you. And you hang in there because you're convinced that you can do a better job as a servant of the people than the guys who want to beat you in the polling places."

The mayor relaxed again, sitting on Mr. Corcoran's desk with one foot dangling.

"It's the same story with every other officeholder in our democratic republic. Sheriffs, assemblymen, senators, or members of the Congress of the United States—and mayors. We all have the same kind of job. Or should have. Working for the best interests of the people. Put in office by the people. And removed from office by the people."

The members of the Rio Bueno High School student

council, the class officers, the thirty students who had signed Philip's original petition, and a dozen others who had shown interest in politics as a career sat quietly as Mayor Martinez told them in crisp, cogent sentences about his office, his staff, and the other elective offices in Rio Bueno.

He entertained them with stories, and alternately had them laughing and solemnly serious. Time evaporated, and the school bell rang too soon—Career Day was officially over.

Ordinarily, when the final bell sounded students ran all over each other trying to clear the building. Today they sat transfixed as Mayor Martinez talked right up to and through the clanging bell.

"Is that it?" he asked Mr. Corcoran.

"Yes it is, Mr. Mayor. The end of the day."

The students remained in their seats, groaning audibly, not wishing to leave. Feet shuffled. The door opened and two students left the room. The others remained, hoping for more from this gifted speaker.

"Time flies," Manuel Martinez said, spreading his hands, palms up. "Sorry we don't have more of it."

"Well, Mr. Mayor," the teacher said, "we could stay a little longer, if you'd like to answer any questions. . . ."

"Oh, yes. Please stay." The request became a chorus.

Mayor Martinez turned to Donald Dixon. "How about it?"

Dixon shrugged. "We have that meeting at five. . . ."

"It's only three now."

"Okay with me." Dixon looked at Mary Lucas. "You have anything else on the calendar?"

"No." Mary Lucas was enjoying the experience and she said so. "No, I think we should stay," she added.

"All right, then," Manuel Martinez said, "how about some questions? Anything in particular I can clear up?"

Hands waved throughout the room and, for the next hour,

the mayor and his aides answered queries of all kinds.
At one point, Steve engaged in a lively exchange with the
mayor.

Q. How did you get the idea you wanted to go into
politics?
A. I got interested in high school, just as you have.
Class office, student body office. Then in college I
became involved in volunteer precinct work. The
next thing I knew, I got some backing for the school
board. I ran, I was elected, and I must have done a
good job, because some people asked me to try for
City Council. Now, here I am, mayor of Rio Bueno.
Q. You make it sound so easy. Didn't you have any
trouble getting elected?
A. Trouble? Politics is nothing but trouble. How about
you? Do you hold an office here at Rio Bueno?

Steve cleared his throat and looked at Gladys. "I'm secretary of the junior class."

"Did you have any trouble getting elected?"

"You know it. I was running against a girl. And I won by
only four votes."

"What were your qualifications?"

A laugh came from the back of the room. "He's a good
dancer." More laughter followed.

Steve said, "I can type. I'm the fastest shorthand taker
in school. And my counselor says I'm well organized."

"Did you get votes for that?"

"Yes. But I had to convince people I could do the job."

"How did you do that?"

"I told them I could."

Mayor Martinez smiled, spread his arms wide, and said,
"That, my friend, is how elections are won."

"But my dad says, when big time elections come around,
it's the money that counts." Steve stood his ground.

"Did your dad also tell you that politicians are corrupt
and unscrupulous?"

Steve turned brick red, but remained firm. "Yes, sir. That's what he said."

"Well, I guess we'll have to do something about that. What's your name, son?"

"Steve."

"Look, Steve, we don't have enough time to go into the cost factors of running a campaign here. And your dad is right. It takes money to get elected. But your dad's wrong on one count. Politicians are not corrupt, per se. Oh, I'll admit there are crooked politicians. So are there dishonest merchants, quack doctors, thieving auto mechanics. Of all the careers to which you were exposed today, not one speaker can say that all the people within that particular profession or trade are inherently honest.

"Everyone has to be his own man," Manuel Martinez continued. "Or woman," he added, taking a quick look in Mary Lucas' direction. "You have to be prepared. If you're running for an office where shorthand is important, and you have that skill, you tell the voters about it. If you are working for the laborers' votes, you learn all you can about the workingman's problems. And you tell the voters about that. If you're representing the farm vote, you learn all there is to know about farming. And if you're going for everyone's vote, across the board, you build a philosophy that will be for the greatest good, and you tell all the people about your philosophy. Some of them will accept it. Some will reject it openly. You hope that enough understand it to back you financially, ultimately work for you, and vote for you. That's all there is to it."

Mayor Martinez paused and surveyed the crowded room. After a moment he spoke again.

"You know, I think there is something wonderful here. First, we have a large group interested in what I as a mayor, an elected official, and a politician, have to say. And you're apparently so interested that you chose to stay after school.

But I feel there is so much that hasn't been said. There is so much for you to learn. Not from me, necessarily, but from others—all officeholders, in every echelon, and their staff. In the state capitol, in Washington, D.C., and in small towns and villages across the country, there are people who can tell you about careers in elective government."

Seeking the teacher's eye, the mayor said, "Mr. Corcoran, how much time do you have before the semester ends?"

Mr. Corcoran did a bit of rapid mental arithmetic and answered, "A little over three months, Mr. Mayor."

The speaker turned his attention back to his audience.

"I'd like to make a recommendation," he said, selecting his words carefully. "Why don't those of you who are really interested form a separate club or society or whatever you wish to name it. As a project between now and the end of the school year, research in depth exactly what elective government means. Write to and visit your state assemblyman and your state senator, and state officials in other states. Go to the district office of your United States representative. Get in touch with your United States senator. Talk to the councilmen, the water commissioner, the Board of Equalization and other tax boards, your own school board trustees— just everyone who relies on the vote of the people to acquire and hold a position."

He swiveled his head. "Mary, can you help with this? A letter of introduction. . . ."

Mary nodded and offered a suggestion. "Perhaps if the students could feel free to come to your office with questions that need answering . . ."

"By all means."

Donald Dixon spoke up. "I have shelves of books they can use for research."

Philip looked troubled. "There must be thousands of people to write to," he said dubiously.

"Hundreds of thousands," the mayor answered. "Don't

expect to write to everyone. But you can figure out the best ones when you meet on this later."

"I have an aunt who lives in Washington. I wonder—how much would it cost me to go and visit her?" Steve asked.

The mayor laughed. "I don't know, several hundred dollars, no doubt. And it would mean missing school."

"I wonder . . ." Steve mused, half to himself.

"There should be some research done on academic preparation," Mr. Corcoran added.

"By all means," the mayor said. "That is a very important area of research. That reminds me of one thing more. I think you will find that people who work in elective government are a little special. They think differently. They are generally more optimistic. You will find them more willing and more helpful than most people working in other occupations. That eagerness may come from their desire to please their constituency; they may seem to you to be constantly running for office. You will be aware of it from the lowest level of staff up to the top. I mention this so you won't be afraid of refusal or rebuff."

The mayor hesitated then, scanned the room, and seemed to memorize each face looking at him.

"Elective government is a good career choice," he said. "And in many instances, the pay is good—very good," he added, laughing. "Well, that's it for today. It's been a real pleasure for me as well as my staff. By the time you finish this project, you'll know more about politics and politicians and elective government than most of the nation's citizens."

Laughing again, and waving his hand flamboyantly, the mayor strode from the room with the same verve with which he had entered.

At the school entrance, the two-man television crew waited.

"No trouble in the school, is there, Mr. Mayor?" the cameraman-reporter asked, hoping for a scoop.

"None at all. On the contrary. Follow me down to City Hall and I'll tell you all about it."

The following day, the Student Council and several dozen interested students met again in Mr. Corcoran's room. A loosely structured club was formed, committees for different elective areas were named, and interview task forces were organized. Letterwriting teams selected correspondents. A trip to the state capitol was tentatively planned. Steve dreamed about going to Washington, D.C.

The Rio Bueno High School Elective Government Club was on its way.

At the close of the semester, fourteen chairpersons assembled their committees' notes, and put them into concise form. Mr. Corcoran bound them in a thick folder and made them a permanent part of his course in elective government.

Chapter

2. A PLAN FOR PREPARATION

"The ability to plan action for which the reward is a long way off is the central thing that the human brain has in which there is no match in animals."

These are the words of the late Dr. Jacob Bronowski, author of *The Long Childhood*, spoken as part of the documentary television series, *Ascent of Man*.

"We are concerned in our early education actually with the postponement of decision," the noted philosopher/anthropologist stated. "We have to put off the decision-making process in order to accumulate enough knowledge as a preparation for the future."

In our research into elective government as a career, it was evident from the outset that we had an inordinate amount of knowledge to accumulate.

The elected representatives themselves offered no proven path along which the novice could most swiftly and safely travel. Each has his or her own motivation, guided by a philosophy often set in "group psychology"—better known as party loyalty.

One lawyer-congressman thinks the business of government can best be conducted by those versed in the law. A cattle rancher won his state senate seat by convincing his constituency (many of whom were farmers and ranchers) that there were too many lawyers in the capitol.

We talked, too, with a lawyer fresh out of school who never dreamed that she'd be working as counsel to a lieutenant governor, and to a mayor who has been an elected official for eighteen years, yet makes one-third the salary of the young lawyer.

It seems that long-range plans have had little to do with the actions of these people. However, it is obvious that each person had accumulated enough knowledge to prepare for the future.

The first thing we learned is the difference between *elective* positions, appointive "exempt" positions, and the Civil Service Merit System of employment within the public sector.

"To Americans who value honest and reasonably efficient government, it comes as a shock to realize there was a time when federal jobs were sold to the highest bidder. . . ."

So writes Robert A. Liston in his book, *Your Career in Civil Service.*

Skillfully Liston traces the history of civil government employment from the days of George Washington when there were 350 civilian employees, through 1835 when the spoils system ran rampant, to the present when over 2.5 million people are employed through the Federal Civil Service Merit Program.

Strong advocates of the Merit System would see all government positions—local, state, and federal—controlled by civil service laws.

An *exempt* status—still referred to by many as "patronage"—allows the elected official to employ persons close to his way of thinking and his basic philosophy.

It is of primary importance, according to elected officials we interviewed, that the aides they appoint are competent individuals, colleagues who can be trusted to undertake major responsibilities.

These positions include secretaries, administrative assistants, legislative aides, researchers, consultants, and special committee staff, on upward to state commissioners, members of the cabinet, and even ambassadors.

All of these positions are exempt and appointive; all depend on the elective office from which they are assigned; and all are within the purview of our study.

We did not concern ourselves in any way with civil service government employment.

However, we were concerned with the point at which *any* organization becomes a *government*.

The latest United States Census of Governments (1972) has this description:

. . . an organized entity which, in addition to having governmental character, has sufficient discretion in the management of its own affairs to distinguish it as separate from the administrative structure of any other governmental unit.

Governmental character means popular elections, taxing powers, and public accountability; *sufficient discretion* refers to administrative independence.

The *organized entity* is one in possession of corporate powers such as ". . . perpetual succession, the right to sue and be sued, have a name, make contracts, acquire and dispose of property, and the like."

At the beginning of 1972, the census shows 78,269 governmental units in the United States. These were divided among:

U.S. Government	1
State Governments	50
Local Governments	
Counties	3,044
Municipalities	18,517
Townships	16,991
School Districts	15,781
Special Districts	23,885
	78,269

Special districts include the most varied of entities: natural resources (soil conservation, drainage, irrigation and water conservation, flood control); fire protection; sewerage; parks and recreation; highways; libraries—literally dozens of small districts indigenous to the agricultural, industrial, and housing patterns of the nation.

The administration and economic control of all these governments depend primarily on over one-half million popularly elected officials.

Add to this total the approximate number of aides employed by the elected official—one million—and you will readily see that there are ample opportunities for one wishing to allot a part or the whole of a career to public service.

The two per cent of the populace who are occupied in elective government—officials and aides—are not the only ones in "the game of politics."

Author Herbert Kaufman (*Politics and Policies in State and Local Government*) doesn't believe anyone is excluded. The game of politics is not a spectator sport, according to Kaufman. Even the observers are drawn into the game.

Both active and passive partake. When a candidate campaigns, reactions occur; when a citizen refuses to register and cast a vote, he or she influences both a neighbor and an office seeker. Like any other game, the better we understand the rules, know the players, and recognize the benefits—the money, prestige, control of policy, and power that come with the office—the more enjoyable the game becomes.

Involvement is the key to participation, if one wishes to classify oneself in the active role. How does one become involved?

Paul Douglass and Alice McMahon tell how in their book *How To Be An Active Citizen*.

Be informed on public issues

Discuss public issues with others
Talk and write about politics
Belong to organizations that take stands on issues
Contribute to a political party or candidate
Work for a political party or a candidate
Vote
Hold office as a private citizen

Douglass and McMahon put emphasis on the part the private citizen can play, in contrast to the elected public official. They offer examples of individuals who have been active in "the office of the private citizen," although none had ever run for elective office:

Susan B. Anthony, the famed and revered instigator of the woman suffrage movement;

Hugh Bentley, a mild-mannered retail store operator who (after the previous president was shot and killed) fearlessly led the Russell County, Alabama, Betterment Association in defeating the vicious gangster vice syndicate which had taken over Phenix City;

Hyman G. Rickover, who in 1947 conceived the feasibility of the atomic submarine, and patiently proceeded to develop his project, overcoming "every bureaucratic roadblock to realize an authentic idea;"

Halford E. Luccock, who never held a public office, yet influenced the thinking of countless preachers and laymen through his chair in homiletics in the Yale University Divinity School, urging citizens to unify human welfare.

It was Dr. Luccock who preached the wisdom of the bear who went over the mountain: One can always see the view from his own side of the mountain; it is necessary to go over the mountain to get the opposite viewpoint.

The history of America is filled with biographies and anecdotes such as these put forth by Douglass and McMahon, telling of citizens who performed great service without benefit of elective office. Thousands more go unheralded, noted only briefly on local scenes.

It is unfortunate that the word "activist" carries with it the connotation "radical." For one can become involved through activism without becoming radical or anarchistic.

Campus radicalism of the sixties with its anger and its violence—although the validity of many of its issues is not refuted—has been replaced by community concerns such as food costs and quality, creditor abuses, dozens of consumer ills, housing, pollution (visual, sound, air, water), education, and transportation.

These concerns, and more, are listed in W. Ron Jones' guide to community research and action titled *Finding Community*, prepared with the help of Julia Cheever and Jerry Ficklin.

One could easily become involved, formally or casually, within as many spheres of interest as one could imagine.

But when policy is to be determined, when laws are to be written, when elections are to be won or lost—these are the exciting arenas of action.

To prepare for the action, a plan must be made to cover all requirements within the "scope" of qualification for any position within elective government.

During the course of our study of elective government and all its tangential occupations, we were continually impressed by the high quality of intellect exhibited by those with whom we met personally. And we were amazed to discover the long hours put in by our elected representatives, in all phases of government.

This does not mean, of course, that there are no people in government who don't belong there. This is why we hold elections.

Our preconceived supposition that the way into elective government is through some long-established route was in error. A degree in political science neither helps nor hinders, taken by itself. Passing the bar examination is not an entree into the legislature without some accessory armament. A college education in business administration, journalism, economics, or sociology will be an excellent basic in your resumé, but is not the main criterion that will help you reach your goal.

To help you plan before you prepare, we queried each elected official and aide with whom we came in contact during the weeks of our research. The following is a distillation of their suggestions as to what steps you, as a potential career-minded student of elective government, should include in your action plan:

1. Practice public speaking; join the debating team, or organize one if none is in your school; run for school office.
2. Sharpen your literary skills through extended reading and writing exercises.
3. Study and learn from American history.
4. Learn to meet people; learn to be gracious; learn to listen; learn when not to speak.
5. Build your mechanical skills, including typing, shorthand; have knowledge of general office machines—mimeograph, photocopiers—and data processing.
6. Make yourself known around political circles by volunteering your services at individual campaign offices, party headquarters, precinct centers.
7. Strengthen your powers of concentration and memory.
8. Study your own state and local election codes; become familiar with their history and provisions.
9. Select your college and your major course of study with care.
10. Don't be naive. Take an academic interest in graft and corruption; be prepared to combat them.
11. Don't be cynical. The need for change should be a challenge, not a turn-off.
12. Stay healthy through intelligent personal habits.

Political life is demanding, and often foreshortened needlessly by poor health.

As an adjunct to education, access to leadership in the administration of government is being made more attainable through public service internships and fellowships, financed at local, state, and federal levels, as well as through private foundations. As an integral link in your plan, internships should be investigated thoroughly.

Frank Logue, in his Ford Foundation Survey and Report *Who Administers*, brings out the appropriative values of internships, stating, "Exposure to the world of the public official is widely regarded as a form of encouragement to enter public service. . . ."

Mr. Logue includes a wide variety of internships within his survey, one or more of which could be a goal in your plan.

Sharlene Pearlman Hirsch has developed the Executive High School Internships Program through a nationwide network of selected school districts, one of which may be yours. If your school district does *not* participate in Dr. Hirsch's program—investigate, become involved!

Mr. Logue's survey included an extra bit of information that seems pertinent at this stage of our report:

The people who interview for prospective placement of interns are instructed to judge interviewees on the following six factors in their evaluation:

Bearing and Manner
Social Adjustment
Ability in Oral Expression
Problem Solving Ability
Motivation and Maturity
Leadership Qualities

The above is a valuable checklist for your own use under any circumstances in which you will face an oral, in-person examination. Try some practice sessions with your friends or with the assistance of a teacher or an interested objective adult.

Another segment of your plan can be titled "Learn the Political Language."

The language of politics and policy making, while it is made of words found in every dictionary, tends to obfuscate—and that's a dandy example right there.

Political language is sprinkled with clichés, but it is also formed with legalese phrases that can only be found within the bounds of the legislature—state and national.

In his book *Political Obligation*, Richard E. Flathman makes two premises governing language usage:

1. that language is governed by conventions
2. that knowing the language consists of knowing the conventions that governs its use.

"If we are going to generalize about the use of language we have to get out of our armchair and investigate the diversity and complexity that is actual use of language," Flathman writes.

In our case, if we are to understand government and policymaking through its language, it is necessary that we participate in that language long enough to become conversant with its usage.

"It is pretty obvious," Flathman declares, "that I cannot rely entirely on my own command of English in giving an account of many of the concepts used in discourse among skydiving buffs or among members of the Black Panther Party. I have to learn how to use many of the concepts they employ; I have to learn how they are used by skydiving buffs and Black Panthers."

Knowing how government works from the inside is valuable to any citizen—learning the concepts and the diversity and complexity of the language.

It is valuable to lawyers as well, as we learned from Harold Himmelman, who is now in private law practice in Washington, D.C.

We first became aware of Mr. Himmelman through Hunter S. Thompson's hilarious and often irreverent book, *Fear and Loathing on the Campaign Trail*. Himmelman was deeply involved with the Ohio phase of Senator George McGovern's ill-fated presidential campaign, and later moved to Washington to work as a legislative aide, and then a civil rights advocate.

We asked Mr. Himmelman, "Do you think it advisable that a young lawyer spend some time within the policy-making sector to gain firsthand experience on the state and/or federal level of legislation?"

Harold Himmelman's answer was an emphatic "Yes."

"There is no doubt in my mind," he told us, "that some experience in government or politics (and preferably both) is helpful in understanding how 'the real world' works. The insights gained in the political arena are invaluable to being an effective advocate."

Whether you prepare for a profession or a position in business or industry, or concentrate totally on a career in elective government, your plan should include the long childhood of accumulation of knowledge.

For you to do now:
Guided by the bibliography and recommended reading list in the back of the book, set aside two titles to be read as soon as possible.

Chapter

3. YOUR OPPORTUNITIES
IN LOCAL GOVERNMENT

What do Kari Rady, who is sixteen and a junior at Newark High School; Atha Mathieu, twelve-year-old seventh grader from San Anselmo; and twenty-one-year-old Joe Canciamilla of Pittsburg, have in common at the time this book is being written with Father Roland H. St. Pierre, Plattsburgh, New York, chaplain and pastor; Ada Evans, a housewife from the only black family in Fairplay, Colorado; and Donald F. Dellmann, a businessman from the tiny lakeside village of Pewaukee, Wisconsin?

All of these individuals are members of one of the 78,218 popularly elected local governing bodies listed in the 1972 Census of Governments.

The first three people are from California. Miss Mathieu and Miss Rady are both members of their home town park and recreation commissions. Mr. Canciamilla is school board president of the Pittsburg Unified District.

The second trio are mayors of the respective city-town-village each calls home.

Atha Mathieu voted against poison-oak removal in her first meeting with the Parks and Recreation Commission. Not a big deal, but a genuine responsibility for a twelve-year-old, because her vote had an impact on the $252,688 city budget under review.

Atha also won a fight for a bigger community building,

which was in line with her original proposal in a letter to the city council in which she said, "Parks are for children, and we need representation," when she applied for the vacant seat of a resigning commissioner.

Kari Rady, also named by her city council to fill a vacancy, was delighted to have the chance to start on what she terms the road to a major political career.

"I've been thinking about politics for a long time," she was quoted in the press. "I'm going to study law, and I'll go on from there."

Miss Rady, active in school sports and music, has plans to organize a youth council to work with the commission.

Joe Canciamilla was elected to the Pittsburg Unified School Board when he was still in high school.

"I had two and a half months between election and graduating," he told radio personality Art Finley during an interview over station KGO, San Francisco. "This presented a problem to some of my last semester teachers, who asked the principal how they should deal with me, how I should be graded."

Adults on school boards and commissions don't always take kindly to teen-age candidates, who offer sometimes startling alternatives to the so-called "tried and true." Establishment adults fear for their capability in handling assets that often top $100 million a year. With experience, however, student-members develop sophistication, not only with budgetary and curricular problems, but with public relations and campaign tactics.

The more than 18,000 United States municipalities have some 143,000 elected officials. To this figure add 75,000 elected in the 3,000-plus counties; 130,000 officeholders in nearly 17,000 townships; and 39,000 school districts and special districts being served by more than 164,000.

That's a lot of people taking care of the public's business on the local level.

What motivates all of these hundreds of thousands to pursue careers in elective government?

Money? Power? Greed?

It hardly seems possible.

With the exception of the office of superintendent of schools, national averages for salaries of elected public officials is somewhat below the norm as set by professionals working within fields adjacent to local public servants. The national all-cities average annual salary:

Mayor	$ 4,000
City attorney	15,000
Controller	15,000
City Manager	18,000
Superintendent of schools	24,000

Harry J. Parrish, mayor of the town of Manassas, Virginia, decries the thought of dishonesty in government, or private gain as a motive for seeking election.

"This is far from the truth," Mr. Parrish answered our query in this regard. "Most elected officials hold office only because they desire to serve and help their fellowman. Particularly in grass roots (local) government, elected officials many times vote for things that may hurt them individually if they are convinced that the action is proper for the majority of their constituents."

Mr. Parrish, who has served the citizens of this historic Prince William County municipality for twenty-three years —twelve as councilman before he became mayor—offers a list of prerequisites he feels necessary for a career in elective government:

1. A strong desire to serve your fellowman and to put the well being of the majority above self interest.
2. While a law degree is not necessary, one must be able to read and understand law.
3. Business experience is desirable, as all government

at all levels is nothing but big business; proper control and use of the taxpayer's dollar is one of the great responsibilities of all elected officials.

4. Academic preparation should include some law, such as business law, some economics, some statistics, and above all, some common sense.

Ada Evans likes her little mining town perched high in the mountain passes of Colorado. Her husband, Ray, is happy teaching music within the school system. Besides its mines, Fairplay boasts a restored ghost town to which it is hoped tourists will be attracted. But little Fairplay, the seat of Park County, has no paved streets.

Paved streets for Fairplay led to public office for Ada Evans.

More and more black citizens like Mrs. Evans are gaining elective offices throughout the nation. As of April 1, 1974, there were 2,991 blacks holding elective positions in 45 states and the District of Columbia, including 120 mayors. Some of the foremost mayors who are black include Kenneth Gibson, Newark; Coleman Young, Detroit; Maynard Jackson, Atlanta; Clarence Lightner, Raleigh; James McGee, Dayton; and Thomas Bradley, Los Angeles.

The salary range on the county level of local government is higher than that of the municipalities:

County population:	over 1 million	50- to 100,000	overall average
Assessor	$30,000	$11,500	$10,000
Sheriff	30,000	11,000	10,000
School superintendent	32,000	20,000	15,500
District Attorney	35,000	15,000	12,000

Only in the nation's six largest cities (over 1 million population) does the mayor receive comparable pay, a median of $37,500.

As a class, counties are primarily agents for carrying out

functions assigned to them by the state. However, "home rule" and "charter counties" with more extensive powers are increasing in number.

"Organized county governments are found throughout the nation, except in Connecticut, Rhode Island, the District of Columbia, and limited portions of other states," it was recorded in the Census.

Outside municipal boundaries, in "county" territory, incorporated areas take on various designations, depending mainly on the state traditions. Alaskan counties are called "boroughs"; Louisiana calls them "parishes."

In Wisconsin the village form of government prevails.

The village board consists of a president (mayor) elected to that office by the voters; six trustees are also elected, and serve "at large" because there are no wards or districts.

The responsibilities of the village board and president are similar to that of mayor-council: they serve as a policy and law making body. Village business is authorized during regular semi-monthly board meetings, always open to the public.

Donald F. Dellmann became president of the village of Pewaukee, Wisconsin, in 1971, after having served as trustee for five terms of two years each.

"I have enjoyed this service very much," Dellmann told us, "and have obtained a tremendous personal satisfaction in this type of work."

This statement wasn't given without a touch of sadness mixed with chagrin: Don Dellmann lost his 1975 election to a write-in candidate when his overconfident supporters stayed home from the polls.

But Don hasn't lost his respect for his office, or the form of government it represents.

"The village form of government is one of the most democratic forms of our municipal governments," he told us. "All citizens have a right to appear before the village board and express any complaints or grievances or suggestions they may have. This is the first order of business at each regularly scheduled meeting. In addition, the village president and all the board members are constantly receiving calls regarding matters that the local citizens would like attended to."

For being constantly "on tap," the president of this small bedroom/resort community—4,000 population, 1,500 registered voters, less than an hour's drive west of the city of Milwaukee—is paid $1,800 a year. Out-of-pocket expenses are reimbursed up to $200. Trustees receive $1,200 plus $50 expenses.

"Each village establishes its own pay schedule," Dellmann said. "There are several large villages in the Milwaukee area where being village president is practically a full time job. In those cases, his pay would be commensurate with the time that was necessary to spend."

Dellmann pointed out that being an ombudsman—a position which is that of individual advocate against the powers, begun in the early 1800s in Sweden—"is one of the more important functions of our job."

In cities nationwide, municipalities are governed by a mayor, who works with a city council in the making of policy. If the mayor has been granted by city charter the sole power to execute that policy, to appoint commissions, and to veto measures passed by the city council, he is in a *strong* mayor position.

Conversely, if the city charter allows the mayor none of the above prerogatives, and counts his vote on issues only as equal to that of the separate council members, he is known to be in a *weak* mayor position. Charters in this case usually call for a city manager to execute policy. The city manager is appointed by the council as a body.

Professional municipal management began in Staunton, Virginia, where a "general manager" was employed in 1908 to watch over the town's public functions.

Four years later, the city council of Sumter, North Carolina, hired a manager, thus becoming the first of many council-manager methods of municipal government.

Dayton, Ohio, is credited for being the first large-sized community to operate under the council-manager plan (1914); Durham County, North Carolina, in 1930, became the first county to hire a professional manager.

The complete story and data of professional municipal management is found in the *Municipal Year Book*, the annual publication of the International City Management Association (ICMA).

According to the 1974 *Year Book*, 2,588 places within the United States were verified by ICMA as operating under the council-manager plan. Included in this total are 168 municipalities, 55 counties, and 44 councils of government (towns, villages, etc.) "recognized" by ICMA on a basis of relevant education and experience, their "general management criteria."

"While professional management is defined by a common set of functions," says the *Year Book*, "the Association has not sought to control entrance into the profession by completion of a specified education program. The primary emphasis for entrance has been on demonstrated competence in a position with significant management responsibility and authority."

Richard H. Marriott is the *weak* mayor of California's capital city, Sacramento.

Dick Marriott, while classified in the "weak mayor" category, is anything but a weak personality.

Marriott, editor of the Sacramento *Labor Bulletin*, spends his mornings in the newspaper office, his afternoons in City Hall, and his evenings attending civic and social functions around the busy capital city.

"How many hours *do* you work?" we asked during a visit to his large, walnut-appointed office.

"It isn't just the hours behind this desk," he answered affably, "it's the total hours in a day. I spend approximately 50 per cent of seven days a week, night and day, functioning somehow in a capacity related to the mayor's office. That means when I'm in the other office, where I earn my living, I am frequently on my phone doing city business."

Do people come there on city business? we wondered.

"Frequently," Marriott answered. He leaned back in his big leather swivel chair, adjusted his glasses, and placed his hands behind his head.

"I also spend a good portion of my time at evening functions," he continued, "that are all related to the mayor's office. In other words, I would not be invited to attend these functions were I not mayor."

He mentioned the Cinco de Mayo celebration held recently, during which the local Mexican-American community held a festival remembering that important Mexican holiday.

"They like to see the mayor there, and of course the mayor likes to join in their activities, and offer his support to their programs."

Mayor Marriott personally enjoys these ceremonial activities, but he thinks the office of mayor of Sacramento should have more importance.

"Many years ago, when I first came into this office, I looked up the meaning of the word *mayor*. Webster's big dictionary says that the mayor is the chief magistrate. And in this community we do not have a chief magistrate. We have a figurehead; a ceremonial kind of thing."

"In other words," we asked him, "you don't really have executive power?"

"None. And it isn't what Dick Marriott personally is looking for. It's what I think the function of government should be in today's world, in a city of this size. Our charter was adopted in 1921. This city has grown eight or ten times larger in population, and the problems have multiplied proportionately."

In the general election of November 5, 1974, the voters of the city and county of Sacramento turned down a new charter that would have consolidated, merged, and incorporated the two separate entities into one city/county, similar to that of nearby San Francisco.

Under the new charter, the mayor would have become the chief executive officer, charged with the duties of preparing the annual budget, appointing members of boards and commissions, seeing that the laws of the city/county were executed, and being the official head of the city/county for all purposes.

The present charter, in which the mayor is only another member of the city council, does not allow the council to take any part in administration, relegating that power to an appointed city manager.

"The charter specifically forbids elected officials of this city tampering with the administration of this government," Mayor Marriott patiently explained. "The council is a policy body. It hires the manager, and once the manager is hired *he* is the chief executive officer. He appoints the chief of police. He appoints the fire chief and all the department heads. And he is responsible for them. The city manager in this city is responsible for the function of this government 24 hours a day, 365 days a year. That's his job. He's paid 40-some thousand dollars for doing it."

Richard Marriott, as mayor, receives a salary of $300 per month, with a flat $150 per month expense account.

Marriott, who strongly favors city/county consolidation for the primary reason of eliminating the overlapping of governmental districts and functions, as well as providing better services for less taxes, would not change the office of the city manager as chief administrative officer.

"It wouldn't be a whit different than it is," he said, with the exception that "he would be appointed by the mayor."

Serving at the pleasure of . . .

This is the term used in government referring to one who is appointed by an elected official.

Such elective local officers as assessor, auditor, district attorney, sheriff, and board of education and community council members may appoint "such assistants and deputies" exempt from civil service as may be provided by ordinance. Each state has its own codes that guide the appointing of aides.

In the city of Sacramento, the mayor's office rates one assistant, Mrs. Luen Fong, who has been Richard Marriott's secretary and chief assistant for eight of the sixteen years she has been in the council office.

We asked Mayor Marriott what preparation would best prepare a student for a career in local government.

"Learn to read and write!" he exploded.

"That's quite emphatic," we smiled.

"You bet!" he said. "And I mean well, in both cases. Read well. And read anything. And everything. And write. Learn how to use the language."

"Is there any college course you would recommend?"

"Anyone who has been through any college curriculum has prepared in some fashion to function in public office. This would be especially true of those who have had legal education. There are many curricula as far as school systems are concerned which give a rounding out to people who might later become an elected official, and I think this is important. But in a large sense, anyone who is elected— whether a person goes into the state legislature or into the nation's Congress—first off, you have to find out how the system works. Then you have to find out what you can do and what you can't do. And there is an important distinction between what you can do and can't do."

"The best way to find out is on the job?"

"That's right."

A postscript must be added here:

Several weeks after our interview, Richard Marriott was appointed to the California State Unemployment Insurance Appeals Board by Governor Edmund G. Brown, Jr. The appointment came as a surprise to Marriott, whose name was already on the ballot for another term as mayor of Sacramento. His new job will pay $34,104 annually, and because it is a full time occupation, Marriott also resigned his position as editor of the *Labor Bulletin*.

John Ray Harrison is the mayor of the city of Pasadena, Texas, which proudly proclaims itself to be the "Industrial Center of the Southwest."

Texas, like California, has codes calling for nonpartisan elections in the local arena. And Harrison, like Marriott, claims Democratic party affiliation.

The two mayors also agree on educational prerequisites for careers in public office.

In answer to our query, the Texan wrote: "Two years of academics, a degree in law, business, or political science" could be adequate academic training. Then Harrison added a thought that underlines all our previous statements:

Politics is the art or science of government. Qualified, far-sighted people are needed to practice the art of government as they are needed to practice the arts and sciences in other fields.

Those who would guide and influence governmental policy need to be honorable men, interested in bettering their community and performing a service to their neighbors.

Some local governments are definitely partisan. Some depend on party loyalties for their strengths. But not Mayor

Roland H. St. Pierre, a former Democrat turned Republican who brought the first Republican administration in thirty-three years into Plattsburgh, New York.

Fighting long-term, civil service-protected patronage in city jobs—one person out of every 70 in the traditionally Democratic city of 18,000 works for the local government—Father St. Pierre pledged not to replace patronage job holders who resign. He was also concerned not only as a priest, but also as a citizen, by the increased flow of drugs across the nearby Canadian border.

We have all become familiar with civic problems in such large cities as New York, Detroit, Chicago, and Philadelphia. The problems are just as real in Newark and San Anselmo, California; Plattsburgh, New York and North Platte, Nebraska; Auburn, Maine and Auburn, Washington.

Perhaps you, as an elected officer, will find it in your future to help the electorate of your local government overcome these on-going, ever-present problems.

For you to do now:
Introduce yourself to one of your local elected officers.
Tell of your interest in elective government.
Ask advice as to preparation.
Offer your help as a volunteer in *any* job available.

4. YOUR PASS INTO THE STATE CAPITOL

When you shift your sights from local government—city, town, county—to state government, the transition may seem overwhelming in the beginning.

Everything seems so much more important, so complex.

The first difference, and the most noticeable, is political party partisanship. Within local governments, nonpartisanship is the rule rather than the exception, as practiced in certain large cities and a few states where partisan politics goes to grass-root levels.

Within state government, however, the *party* often is the hidden power, despite claims to the contrary by both "ins" and "outs" (majority-minority partisans).

Another difference between state and local government is the sectionalism found in the capitol. Each elected official comes bearing mandates as set forth by his constituency and his own platform. In local government, more of a parochial effort is evident since all local citizens share common goals with neighborly ties.

In state government, for the first time, you may find your future influenced more by philosophies than personalities. If you seek an assembly seat or a place in the state senate, you will depend on those who share your viewpoints and your political theories to taste victory.

Loyalty is a prime factor in receiving assignments. If you

sign on as administrative aide, or staff researcher, or seek assignment to a state board or commission, you will be loyal to the office that assigned you.

If you are of what is considered "liberal Democrat" persuasion, be sure to align yourself with other liberal Democrats. If you share the philosophy of conservative Republicans, seek them out. If you find yourself in concert with a minority party—Libertarians, Prohibitionists, Socialist Workers, Communists: all legal parties within our Constitution—you may find it more difficult to find a niche in the capitol, unless you can build a strong following through the system and convince the voters that you—or your candidate—will best represent them in their state capitol.

Opportunities in state government come under several headings:

> Executive
> Legislative
> Judicial
> Executive and Legislative Staff
> Agencies, Boards, and Commissions

The first two categories are elective. The judicial is appointive and reaffirmed through election.

The others all *serve at the pleasure of the elected.*

When the elective office finds itself with a new "tenant" because of voter preference, the other jobs associated with the office are vacated simultaneously.

One person who has stayed through the tenure of four governors, both Democratic and Republican, and has been reappointed by a fifth is Jackie Habecker, whose official title is "receptionist" in the office of the governor of California.

Jackie Habecker is the first person the literally thousands of visitors to the governor see when they walk through the wide open double doors on the first floor of the capitol annex.

Jackie—a brightly smiling woman who was first hired by Governor Earl Warren—is a living glossary of what goes on within the inner sanctum of the governor's office. When one wants to know how many are to be at a scheduled meeting, Jackie has the information down to the number of chairs ordered. The governor's daily appointment book is at her elbow. If one wishes to go through one of the electronically locked doors leading to the governor's private suite, it is Jackie Habecker who pushes the button.

Through it all, greeting common citizens with the same cheerful welcoming expression she has for visiting dignitaries from Washington, D.C., Jackie remains cool and imperturbable, despite the often hectic atmosphere within the outer office.

"I started as a file clerk," Jackie told us between telephone calls coming through her console. "Back there." She motioned toward a door through which a constant stream of aides and clerks came and went. "One day they needed a receptionist in a hurry. I've been here ever since."

For a receptionist to be reappointed from one administration to its successor, and from one party affiliation to another, says something about how Jackie Habecker handles her responsibilities. After Governor Warren left on his way to the Chief Justice bench of the United States Supreme Court, Jackie stayed on through the administrations of Goodwin J. Knight, Republican; Edmund G. (Pat) Brown, Democrat; Ronald Reagan, Republican, and now, Edmund G. (Jerry) Brown, Jr., Pat's son, another Democrat.

Her latest "boss" has her working hardest, Jackie admits. As a state employee exempt from civil service regulations, her hours are long and unpredictable. Brown, a bachelor who lives in an apartment across Capitol Park from his office, has become notorious for working late at his desk.

"Are you required to stay until the governor leaves?" we asked.

"Only if someone is expected. Then I should be here to meet them."

Further questions brought out the fact that Jackie Habecker had worked until after 11 P.M. twice that week.

"Do you really like a job with such long and irregular hours?" we wondered.

"Oh, yes." Jackie Habecker smiled the same smile that has made her so pleasant to have around the California governor's office since her early file-clerk days. "I love it!"

On a national scope, all elective state offices are salaried—some states pay more, some less. Perquisites, those welcome extras such as per diem expenses, automobile leases, and gasoline credit cards, add to the remuneration.

Some of the elected officers' appointees receive only expenses for their time and effort. These people usually meet only occasionally, and include members of such commissions as conservation, and park and recreation.

Other appointments are full-time commitments, and the individuals receive salaries from $1,000 to more than $3,000 per month.

The latter require some expertise, although it is fairly well recognized that commissions are sometimes chaired by political appointees with no knowledge whatsoever of the field which they regulate.

How does one acquire one of these important assignments?

Perhaps the following information will help:

In September, 1974, the California Legislature's Joint Committee on Legal Equality completed a study and offered a summary on appointment opportunities.

Included in their findings was a section titled: "How to Get Appointed."

Designed for the California electorate, the information made available should be valuable in any state.

"The best way to get appointed is to know the Governor," is the unabashed advice offered the candidate for a commission post.

"If you are politically active, it is going to be a help. When you volunteer your time and money, be sure the candidate knows who you are. Failing a close personal relationship, make sure to get to know a close aide."

Instructions continue in the summary:

Prepare a resume if you don't already have one. List all professional and job-related activity. List all organization memberships, irrespective of seeming relevancy to the particular position being sought. List business and personal references. Include paid and unpaid experience.

Write a letter to the Governor or other appointing power, asking for the position you have selected. Clearly state the reasons why you should be appointed.

Solicit letters of support from elected officials, from organizations, and from people prominent in the community.

Request support from persons knowledgeable in the area of concern, of the board or commission to which you hope to gain an appointment.

Even if you don't know your state legislators or local officials, go to see them, particularly the ones who are of the same political persuasion as the Governor or other appointing power. Inform them of your community involvement and your background that helps fit you for the position desired, and ask them to support your candidacy.

Prepare a rough draft of a letter that you wish your sponsor to send to the Governor or other appointive power. Be sure it is correctly addressed to whomever you wish to receive it.

Remember that when the appointments are being considered, you need a spokesperson to introduce your name as a candidate. If it is a hotly-sought-after post, you will not be considered if you haven't found a champion within the inner circle!

A few of the more than 2,200 commission, agency, and departmental appointments in the state of California—typical of other states as well—selected at random are:

Chief, Division of Apprenticeship Standards	$2,379 per month
Director, Office on Aging	3,066 per month
State Architect	31,128 per year
Director, Alcoholic Beverage Control	33,960 per year

The above represent positions subject to senate approval, and the appointees serve at the pleasure of the governor.

It might be easier to receive an appointment to a commission not so "hotly-sought-after" to gain experience before trying to qualify for the more lucrative appointments. These might include:

State Hospital Advisory Board	Expenses only
Council on Intergovernmental Relations	Expenses only
Manpower Services Council (meets quarterly)	Expenses plus $28 per diem

In all states, but more evident in such largely populated ones as New York, Illinois, Ohio, and California, thousands of appointed positions change hands at the change of administrations. While the exact number of commission, board, and agency jobs are a matter of public record, together with salaries, and certain executive staff positions are also well known and on the record, the total number of aides and the total payroll within the executive branch of state governments is seldom known.

A few at-random selections within the California governor's staff, with annual salary, include:

Special assistant for legislation dealing with
    public employee collective bargaining $34,536
Chairman, State Housing and Community
    Development Department   31,008
Director of the State Department of Motor
    Vehicles   37,212
Director of the Office of Planning and
    Research   34,104
Deputy Appointments Secretary   24,000

In fairness to the recipients in these categories, many are highly qualified personnel—professors, lawyers, economists, bankers—who forego lucrative, on-going careers in the private sector paying much more, to be of service to the "patron" and the public.

Even with such highly qualified people, Governor Edmund G. Brown, Jr., presents a thirteen-page questionnaire—on a confidential basis—to every prospective appointee. Everything from prescribed medications to adverse allegations in the media is covered by the document.

Considering the exhaustive screening of Brown's cabinet members, and the implied competency of appointment candidates, one would think that selections would have come easily. But Brown went outside the candidate list in at least one case.

One who was completely surprised by the governor's offer of a cabinet post was Claire Dedrick, the Secretary of the California Resources Agency, who will have much to say about how many trees are harvested from the state's vast forestlands, and how the water that courses from the Sierra Nevada will be distributed, and about the viability of the new Energy Resources program.

"It just never occurred to me to seek the position," she told reporters who shared her astonishment at her appointment. Mrs. Dedrick, at forty-four the second oldest of Jerry Brown's young staff, holds a distinguished background in political, conservationist, and scientific circles.

She campaigned for Pete McCloskey when he defeated Shirley Temple Black for the Republican nomination to Congress; she was campaign manager for Democratic State Senator Arlen Gregorio; she is a former vice-president of the politically strong Sierra Club; she helped form the San Francisco Bay Conservation and Development Commission; she was employed as a researcher in microbiology at Stanford University, the field in which she holds her doctorate.

All of which proves that the office sometimes seeks the person—but don't depend on it!

It is acutely necessary to fill posts such as the above, and fill them with the best people available. State government must continue to function at the highest possible level of efficiency. Any obsolete or dispensable offices are quickly eliminated by tax-conscious administrations. It is up to the elected executive to show the way.

James Longley, a young and unique Independent, called on eighteen to twenty-five year old college students to help him gain the Maine governor's chair. He is a successful businessman who felt that fiscal responsibilities and liberal humanitarianism had equal priority within his state.

Patrick J. Lucey, the Democratic Wisconsin governor, gave up the governor's mansion in favor of his own house. Savings: $50,000 a year.

Massachusetts Governor Michael S. Dukakis takes the bus to work, chatting with his constituency along the way. The young Democrat also has decreed that dozens of state officers can no longer drive around in government cars.

Republican Robert D. Ray has cut deeply into Iowa's $300 million budget, refusing to take on any new projects.

Regardless of state or status, governor's salaries vary widely. New York pays $85,000, California $49,000; Maryland hits the middle average with $25,000, while Virginia pays $35,000, and Arkansas a relatively low $10,000.

The legislative branch of state government is a world apart from the executive branch and its agencies, boards, and commissions.

It is also a world apart in the area of compensation.

State representatives, assemblymen, and senators have almost always been comparatively underpaid—although voters have historically claimed they receive much more than they are worth. Alexis de Tocqueville, in his classic *Democracy in America*, first published in 1835 following a protracted tour of the burgeoning new nation, pointed out that salaries paid its elected officials seemed to "decrease as the authority of those who receive them is augmented." He held that the public in lower financial circumstances were willing to pay the secondary official more because of a feeling of kinship with him, but higher officials arouse envy.

What other condition could cause a Rhode Island state representative to worry about not having been eligible to collect his unemployment benefits?

Rhode Island pays its legislators $300 for each 60 day session of its legislature. Raymond Moan, from Providence, a blue-collar truck driver, was laid off from his job. Because of his legislator's stipend, he became ineligible for unemployment benefits while his state legislature was in session.

But things aren't that bad all over.

New York granted its lawmakers $23,500 early in 1975. New Yorkers, depending on their leadership posts and ranking on committees, receive premium pay increases ranging from $3,500 to $18,000. Most collect about $5,000 premium pay, and also get a daily expense allowance averaging $3,000 annually.

New York Assemblyman Daniel Haley, after a nationwide personally conducted study of the states' legislatures, concluded that the wide-open manner in which the California legislature conducted its business rated it as tops in the country.

"Public participation is taken for granted in California in legislative committee hearings. In New York it is unheard of," he told reporters. He gave credit for this to the 1911–1917 terms of California Governor Hiram Johnson, who through the recall, referendum, and initiative process made elected officials more responsive to the electorate.

However, for nearly a half-century after Johnson, the California legislature was grossly underpaid, it lacked adequate staffing, it had no paid researchers or facilities, and it was a sitting duck for Arthur H. (Artie) Samish, the liquor lobbyist who bragged that he was "the governor of the legislature."

Today a member of the California legislature receives $23,230, plus $30 per day expenses, plus a $225 automobile leasing allowance, plus a credit card for telephone, gasoline, and automotive services.

"Too much!" cry the voters.

Yet they fail to take into consideration that the legislator is putting in a twelve to fifteen hour day, concentrating on bills that include such diverse subjects as collective bargaining for public employees to mass transit to no-fault auto insurance to education.

And the legislator is expected to be an expert on each.

If the representative's home is far from the capital city, two residences must be maintained; the family may be with the legislator or they may be left behind in the home district. In either case, because the representative must make the weekly commute to cover the home constituency, he or she lives two domestic lives.

Keeping in mind that almost all present day state legislators are professional men or women, or business people successful in their own fields, we wondered what inspired them to leave their livelihood and the comforts of home to journey to state capitols and debate policy for constituents who may be questioning their worth in salaries and talents.

Walk down the corridors of any state capitol.

The doors leading to the legislator's offices are open. Enter and introduce yourself. Ask to meet your representative. He or she may be out—in caucus, in committee, or on the floor of the Assembly or Senate.

There may be one or two people waiting ahead of you, constituents or legislative advocates. The chairs are comfortable, the atmosphere pleasant, the scene busy as phones ring continuously, typewriters click, staff members come and go, people leave messages, pick up messages, disappear through unmarked doors into mysterious back rooms.

If you stay long enough, you will discover that these back rooms are where much research is done, where constituent problems are solved, letters written, speeches composed, and serious consultations take place.

On our tour we took an elevator to the top of the California Capitol's Annex, the East Wing, to what is commonly known as "the penthouse." We went through a door marked Assembly, 29th District, Robert P. Nimmo. A secretary ushered us into Mr. Nimmo's small but cheerful walnut-paneled office, and he stood to offer us a hand in greeting. He seemed genuinely glad to see us, although we were not from his district.

"I had been a member of the county and state Republican committees," Nimmo answered our "why are you here?" query. "Committee friends urged me to run. I had mixed emotions about it, but decided if that was their wish and their judgment, to go ahead and run. And that's how I got here."

As simple as that?

Not quite. Nimmo, a greying man, tall, slender, is better known as Col. Robert P. Nimmo, former Commanding Officer at Camp San Luis Obispo, and more recently United States Property and Fiscal Officer for California.

Born of a pioneer ranching family, Nimmo majored in

animal husbandry before becoming a World War II bomber pilot. Portraits of his three lovely blonde daughters smile down from his office walls. He is a warm, friendly, family man, with no ambitions for national prominence.

"In the last twenty years," he remarked, "I've been in and out of the national capitol and Pentagon innumerable times. The less time I could spend there, the happier I'd be."

Here we met a state legislator with but one thought in mind: to represent his constituency in matters most urgent to them. In Mr. Nimmo's district, these included taxes (too high) and freedom for agriculture and ranchers(too little).

After leaving Assemblyman Nimmo's office, we descended one floor to visit with another rancher, Senator Clare L. Berryhill, of Modesto, in the heart of California's Great Central Valley.

"Why? Well, there has been almost a total lack of agricultural representation in the senate," Berryhill answered our question. "There were twenty-five attorneys up here, and I thought an ag-man belonged here."

Senator Berryhill is, as Nimmo, a family man. In fact, he gives full credit to his wife and five children for their part in his campaign, which covered 60,000 miles of motor-home travel up and down the rugged western slope of the Sierra range, from Yosemite north to the Oregon border.

"I could never have done it without my family," the senator stated, and we believed him.

Motivations are many among those who seek elective office and those who seek appointments at state level to work for them. Age, experience, business and professional status have little to do with incentive, however.

Robbin Lewis felt something lacking in education, and to correct what she thought might be the key to the problem, she asked California Superintendent of Public Instruction Wilson Riles for an appointment to a commission to study and make recommendations for intermediate and secondary education. The commission held forums throughout the state. Robbin Lewis, as part of the commission, found her instincts had been correct. Uppermost, the commission found, was a lack of emphasis on the English language.

"Students really aren't taught composition," she insisted. "Many can't write simple essays, and that is a necessary skill in looking for a job."

Robbin Lewis, when she was appointed to the commission, was sixteen years old, a senior in high school.

For you to do now:
Visit the district office of your state representative, assemblyman, or senator.
Ask which committee would be available for you to work on.
Talk to the administrative assistant in the office.
Visit your state capitol at your earliest opportunity, and call on your representative, assemblyman, or senator.
Visit the legislative chambers and watch the legislature in action.

Chapter

5. YOUR TICKET TO WASHINGTON, D. C.

Your first impression of Washington, D.C., will depend a great deal on what time of the year you go.

Summer visitors—unless they are from the Gulf Coast or the Great Lakes basin, where the climate is similar—will find it oppressively hot and humid. As in too many urban areas, inner-core housing is decrepit and depressing, side streets and alleyways are dirty, traffic patterns often confusing.

In winter the weather ranges from too cold to vaguely springlike.

In *High on Foggy Bottom* Charles Frankel wrote, "The Founding Fathers wanted a city that would belong neither to the North or to the South. They got what they wanted, and we still have it—a capital too far north to escape the snows, and too far south ever to be prepared for them, a neutral, in-between place, of mixed styles and uncertain tastes, where magnolias bloom in the slush."

President John F. Kennedy was quoted as calling the capital "a city of Southern efficiency and Northern charm," which says little for the city, its efficiency, or its charm.

One thinks of Washington as a huge place, and indeed it is if one takes into consideration the "bedroom communities" in neighboring Maryland and in Virginia across the Potomac River.

But the major center of federal government activity can be walked with less effort than it takes to cover eighteen holes on the average golf course. A straight line down The Mall to the Washington Monument is only a mile from Capitol Hill; it is less than two miles from the Capitol to the Lincoln Memorial, and the White House is even closer down Pennsylvania Avenue.

A stroll down Constitution Avenue from 1st to 23rd would take you past the United States District Court, the National Art Gallery, the Federal Trade Commission, the National Archives, and the Museums of Natural History and History and Technology; you'd pass The Ellipse (the big back yard of the White House) and you'd skirt the parklands that surround the Monument and the Memorial. And you'd have strolled less than two miles.

Where policymakers percolate and power pressure-cookers build steam, however, is on each end of this most important mile of urban real estate called Pennsylvania Avenue —the Capitol and the White House.

The people-and-issue-oriented activities ebb and flow with the sessions of Congress; the executive branch with its cabinet and agencies of the United States government in its often adversary role tests the wisdom of the people's elected representatives, who in turn sit in cautious discretion pondering the wisdom of the people "down town."

Surrounding the Capitol are the offices of the Congress: The Rayburn Building, the Longworth and Cannon Buildings on Independence; the Senate Office Buildings on the north side of The Hill.

The executive branch, which includes the White House Office, Bureau of the Budget, National Security Council, Aeronautics and Space Control, cabinet offices, and all the major independent agencies (see chart on page 70) make their base of operation mainly between Capitol Hill and the Potomac River.

THE EXECUTIVE BRANCH

The President

The White House Office

Bureau of the Budget	National Aeronautics and Space Council	National Security Council
Office of Economic Opportunity	Office of Emergency Planning	Office of Science and Technology
Council of Economic Advisers	Office of the Special Representative for Trade Negotiations	

Department of State	Department of the Treasury	Department of Defense	Department of Justice
Department of Health, Education and Welfare	Department of Housing and Urban Development		
Department of Agriculture	Department of Commerce	Department of the Interior	
Department of Transportation	Department of Labor		
Post Office Department			

Major Independent Agencies

Arms Control and Disarmament Agency	Federal Deposit Insurance Corporation	Interstate Commerce Commission	Selective Service System
Atomic Energy Commission	Federal Home Loan Bank Board	National Aeronautics and Space Administration	Small Business Administration
Civil Aeronautics Board	Federal Mediation and Conciliation Service	National Labor Relations Board	Smithsonian Institution
District of Columbia	Federal Power Commission	National Mediation Board	Tax Court of the United States
Export-Import Bank of Washington	Federal Reserve System	National Science Foundation	Tennessee Valley Authority
Farm Credit Administration	Federal Trade Commission	Railroad Retirement Board	United States Civil Service Commission
Federal Communications Commission	General Services Administration	Securities and Exchange Commission	United States Information Agency
			United States Tariff Commission
			Veterans Administration

Of all the people within the executive branch, the only man holding an elective office is the president.

All the rest—the advisors, cabinet members, assistants to the president, directors and associate directors, counsellors, counsels, secretaries—*serve at the pleasure of the president.*

Donald Rumsfeld, Chief Assistant to the President in 1974–75, sought to put the White House Office into perspective when he devised an Organizational Chart that named each position, down to the last deputy and secretary. The Chart (the first ever done by any executive staff) was obsolete almost before he presented it, complete with telephone book, at a press conference.

Speaking of the White House telephone directory, Mr. Rumsfeld said, "By popular demand we are releasing a White House telephone book . . . probably accurate today. I cannot swear to that, but I think it is probably accurate today. It will probably be inaccurate tomorrow."

When referring to the transitory nature of executive staff telephones, Donald Rumsfeld was reliving personal experience, for his own career epitomizes the kaleidoscopic tenure of elected officials and those who work for them. His experience illustrates how many times, and how many different responsibilities, one person must be able to accept if he or she plans a career in elective government.

A former U. S. Navy aviator and flight instructor, Rumsfeld began his Washington career in 1958 when he was Administrative Assistant to Representative David Dennison of Ohio; in 1959 he became Administrative Assistant to Robert P. Griffin of Michigan. In 1960 he was elected to Congress from Illinois' 13th (north of Chicago) District. He was a member of the Government Operations, Science and Astronautic, and Joint Economic Committees.

Leaving Congress, Mr. Rumsfeld became a member of the president's Cabinet from May, 1969, to February, 1973, during his service as Director of the Office of Economic Opportunity and Assistant to the President (May 1969-1970); he was previously Counsellor to the President.

He served as Director of the Cost of Living Council from January, 1971, after a stint with the Property Review Board, of which he was also chairman.

On September 29, 1974, Donald Rumsfeld again became an assistant to the president as Coordinator and head of White House Operations. Just prior to his appointment as Chief Assistant to President Ford, from February 2, 1973, he was U. S. Permanent Representative on the Council of the North Atlantic Treaty Organization with the rank and status of ambassador.

And ultimately Donald Rumsfeld was to cross the Potomac to become Secretary of Defense, with offices in the Pentagon. There is little doubt that this will not be his final berth in Washington.

Each president forms his base of operation to suit himself. No criteria have been offered, although a certain similarity is found under each succeeding administration. The approach of the executive, his working style, is demonstrated by his organization, reflecting his concept of leadership and management of the executive branch of the government.

Rumsfeld introduced the 1974-75 Organization Chart with this statement:

> It is designed with several objectives in mind. First, to provide Cabinet Officers and agency heads and Members of Congress and senior staff members with an opportunity to deal with the President as is necessary . . . to see that the White House, itself, is an effective working part of the government and does not get separated—either the individuals or the institution—from either the rest of the Executive Branch or the Congress or the country.

Although having reduced the total White House staff by approximately 10 per cent in size, Rumsfeld thought it appropriate to add the position of "Deputy" to those offices that work directly with the president.

We felt that it would be desirable if the principal people on the staff did in fact have a deputy . . . an individual who was personally used to working with the President, and with whom the President was used to working. An individual who, when a meeting was called, in the event the principal in that office was not available to be there could fill in so that the work of the Government could go on.

Pointing out that the White House staff numbered 540 when the president assumed office in 1974, Rumsfeld reported that the final number would be under 500.

An Executive Assignment System has been devised by the Civil Service Commission to furnish the president and his agencies competent and experienced personnel. The inventory, mostly highly ranked Civil Service employees of grades GS-15 through GS-18, numbers some 20,000 persons. However, civil service ranking is not necessary to join the White House staff.

Often specialized requirements are mandated when certain subjects are under consideration within the executive branch. At these times, outside consultants, not included on the Organization Chart, are called in to solve specific problems. Personnel already on the rolls of a department or agency in the government—*detailees*—are also brought in to the White House for specific purposes. Detailees, when they stay for more than six months, should be put on White House rolls, according to Rumsfeld.

"If a new function begins and you do not have the authorization or the people, you detail from departments and agencies where they have competence in that area, get the thing started, and then go to The Hill for an appropriation for that function."

The decision-making process within the United States government is by necessity loosely woven. The Organization

Chart was not designed to make a pattern for presidential decision-making. It simply makes the president aware of the principal people dealing with various subjects and issues that may arise.

Donald Rumsfeld had this to say about presidential decision-making:

> In our country, you lead by consent, not by command, and that means that during the period of decision-making if you decide that consent needs consultation, which it almost always does, that means that you have to begin to test those ideas in a marketplace of some sort, and it may involve extensive consultations within the bureaucracy. It may involve extensive consultations with Congress. It may indeed in some instances, such as the economic summit (September, 1974) involve rather extensive consultations in a fairly public way as you move toward your judgments, because your judgments may in some instances depend not only on what you might think in a vacuum but also what you might think would be achievable in the event that the accomplishment of what you are trying to move toward requires the full cooperation of some other sector of the society, or some other branch of the Government.
> There is no formula for how a Presidential decision gets made. There cannot be. There should not be.

Except on rare occasions when the president may issue an executive order, the White House needs legislation to see its philosophy fulfilled. Regardless of its research facilities, its army of researchers, its experienced staff, its cabinet and agencies, nothing moves without congressional action.

Congress, at the same time, must do an extremely adept balancing act as it thrusts and parries within its own domain.

"The United States Congressman has two principal functions," wrote Robert Bendiner in *Obstacle Course on Capitol Hill*, "to make laws and to keep laws from being made. The first of these he and his colleagues perform only with sweat, patience, and a remarkable skill in the handling of creaking machinery; but the second they perform daily, with ease and infinite variety."

The amount of mental pushing and shoving, physical attention to "handling" legislation and passing and defeating bills, plus trips back to the home district to deal with constituent problems, all add up to a tremendous load for any individual to bear.

Donald Riegle was twenty-eight when first elected to the House from Michigan's 7th District. He was still a relatively young man when he confided the following to his diary as he sat alone in his office late one afternoon six years later.

The job takes such an enormous toll, mentally and physically, that it's hard to maintain the pace I set in 1966 and have tried to keep up ever since. As I get older I find myself doing the same things over and over again: trips to the District, constituent office hours at shopping centers, office work, speeches, the unending shuffle back and forth between the office and the House floor to answer quorum calls and vote, the endless commitments to do things and be places. I still feel enthusiastic and committed to the idea of public service, especially if I can help someone or get something done. That's the basic part of me. Knowing I'm going to bat for 500,000 people back home keeps me revved up. But the job is draining my life away. I feel I'm being used up, consumed.

The executive branch keeps long hours too, although perhaps not quite with the sense of commitment as exhibited by Representative Riegle. More than one president has kept his people on twenty-four hour alert, and the attrition level in the White House and Executive Office Building is abnormally high, as compared with the private sector.

However, the pay scale is not picayune, although most associated with the executive and legislative branches, both elected and subordinate, can demand and get as high or higher salaries outside of government.

In the area of compensation the position of president of the United States would be hard to top:

His salary is $200,000, taxable; he receives $50,000, taxable, to assist in defraying expenses resulting from official duties, such as entertaining visiting dignitaries; he gets an additional $40,000, non-taxable, for travel and incidental expenses, and after his term is over his pension amounts to $60,000, with franking (free mail) privileges; he receives free office space, and $65,000 to defray office expenses.

The President's Cabinet is paid $63,000 (taxable) and the vice-president, whose duties center between legislative and executive, receives $65,600, plus $10,000 expenses, all taxable.

Members of Congress receive equal pay, $44,600 annually. Salary, however, is only part of the members' benefits. Under the heading *perquisites* are listed funds designated to make their lives, if not easier, at least more bearable:

Free office space, telephone and telegraph service while in Washington; cash allowances for stationery and rent, as well as telephones in their District and State offices; health insurance discounts; life insurance at discounted premiums; free medical care while at work, including physical examinations, laboratory work, electrocardiograms, ambulance service, and prescribed medicines.

Added fringe benefits include recreational facilities, free parking, transportation to and from home districts, and franking privileges. Junketing travel abroad on "government business" is also included in plus-benefits that come with congressional office. All "perks" can total $488,505 a year.

From the office of the president to the other end of Pennsylvania Avenue, each elected office is a difficult position to hold, and the wages seem often inadequate, even within these relatively exalted levels.

As difficult as the congressman's job seems, however, it would be unworkable within the present scope of government were it not for the aides. Each representative is authorized to employ from 15 to 16 staff assistants, depending on the size of his or her district, to work in either the home office or the Washington office. The representative signs vouchers for from $141,492 to $148,896 annually to pay aide's salaries, which range from $8,000 to $20,000, and more.

Senators' payrolls, with no limitations as to the number of aides, can run as high as $1 million, again depending on the size of the state. It is not unusual for senators to pay top aides as much as $37,500, or more.

Who are these aides?

The researcher, who strives to keep the member's font of knowledge filled concerning legislation introduced by the executive (who has already had his research completed by his White House staff). The researcher must continually feed information to the member for use in formulating judgments and preparing legislation.

The executive secretary, who keeps the office humming in orderly fashion; the constituent mail expediters; the speechwriters; the legislative assistants and administrative aides; the caseworkers both in Washington and in the home district.

These are the indispensable people within all areas of elective government. They are even more important in the nation's capitol and in the White House, and are, in fact, your surest ticket to Washington, D.C.

For you to do now:
Visit your United States representative.
Tell him or her of your plans to enter a career in elective government.
Offer your services.
If you live near Washington, D.C., visit your senator.
Get to know your congressman's aides.

Chapter

6. THE JOB OF THE LEGISLATIVE RESEARCHER

The president of the United States doesn't know everything.

Neither does a governor. Nor a mayor. Nor sheriffs, senators, or members of the House of Representatives.

Despite their sometimes pompous campaign utterances, all of our elected officials are simply human, with limited expertise on most subjects.

What happens then when a constituency calls for some new legislation, or change of statute, or redress of grievances?

In earlier times, when our government was in its formative stage, village elders, selectmen, and some relatively successful businessmen, together with those who had "read the law," were relied upon to make decisions, based on their own experience, to keep the civil gears meshing smoothly. Many of these decisions involved matters of no great importance, but rather dealt with relatively minor problems.

Compare these mundane matters with the decisions that must be made in every town, city, and state as the United States begins its third century of self-government:

Shall the elementary school district raise its budget by $20 million, creating a bond issue, to build two new schools?

Shall the city council vote for a nuclear reactor to supply electric power for a growing metropolis?

Shall the office of the governor enter into a deadlock between medical doctors, insurance companies, and trial lawyers, brought on by an exploding proliferation of malpractice suits?

Shall the president veto a piece of legislation designed to protect the environment against the ravages of strip-mining?

Most congressmen, state legislators, and city officials are well-read individuals. Each has the ability to pick up threads of conversation on a wide variety of subjects. They listen to their constituent visitors, ask questions in a manner that indicates keen interest, and go out of their way to investigate and observe at first hand; they are generous with their time and efforts in conducting hearings, and are usually eager to get to the heart of a vexing problem.

But, as we know, lack of time is often the elected representative's greatest burden. He or she needs aides to share that burden.

Perhaps the most anonymous people in the nation are certain aides to elected public officialdom: a congressional liaison man working out of the White House; an administrative assistant far up in the rural Michigan peninsula; an assemblywoman's executive secretary. The voting public seldom knows of the existence of these people.

This is done by design, however. The aide must always be imbued with a "passion for anonymity," a close confidant to the office which employs him or her, one who "thinks like the boss thinks."

Some aides are even more anonymous than others. They seldom get into the give and take of bill management. They almost never see the floor of the Senate or the House or the state assembly. Their names are never found in local newspapers or glossy national weeklies.

Yet they are among the most important members of any staff.

They are the *researchers*.

The job of the legislative researcher is to supply all necessary data on a given subject, imparting all opinions, pro and con, to his principal, to be used in either defeating or successfully passing legislation.

So-called "bad laws" see daylight because the adversary research was incomplete. Much-needed legislation remains "off the books" because of incomplete, faulty, or nonrecorded data. Legislation can be passed, signed into law, and set aside to gather dust by a noncooperative administration, because the electorate had not insisted on implementation, for lack of research capability and resultant publicity.

Legislative research has much in common with investigative reporting; in the last instance, however, the research follows the deed, in an effort to inform an interested readership of some flaw in government.

Some legislative researchers double as secretaries. Others when called upon may do casework (handling constituent problems) and answer constituent mail. Lawyers, freshly graduated, do research while learning government at its source.

But all good researchers have these characteristics in common: They are inquisitive, they are creative, they are patiently tireless, and they know their way around a library.

As a researcher, you may study the effects of predators on fur-bearing rodents for your assemblyman. Or the subject may be the feasibility of permanent housing for vagrant alcoholics for your city council.

Or, you may research a subject like *Assignment of Medical and Other Health Personnel to Critical Need Areas*, as Eric Redman did.

This was the actual name of a new section of Public Law 91-623, 91st Congress, Senate Bill 4106, the writing and passing of which inspired young Rick Redman to write an engrossing and eye-opening book, *The Dance of Legislation*.

Redman worked for one year in the office of Senator Warren G. Magnuson, a Democrat from the state of Washington, between his graduation from the University of Washington and a year spent at Oxford, England, as a Rhodes Scholar.

During his year as an aide (he had spent the previous summer in D.C. as a student intern), much of Redman's time was taken up by the above bill, the brainstorm of political activist Abraham B. Bergman, M.D., a Seattle pediatrician who was concerned by the lack of medical service in rural and disadvantaged areas.

It was Rick Redman's duty to research the ramifications of the public law, and find out how best to word the amendment. He also had to report on the exact medical situations within the diverse areas covered by the law.

With Redman's help, the bill was "danced" through Congress and became a law.

As a fact-conduit, you, the researcher, may be called upon for a variety of answers, to be ready at a moment's notice to start the telephone dial whirring to fill in a blank space in your superior's portfolio on an important piece of legislation.

If you have been assigned to a committee, you may be handed a task so complex that, when completed, enough material will remain to write a doctoral thesis.

You may begin your research job in a congressional office, such as that of Bella S. Abzug, Representative from New York's 20th district.

If you were an experienced researcher, you would have been very welcome in Mrs. Abzug's Rayburn Building office (she has since moved to the Longworth Office Building), when she began her first year in Congress.

On January 20, 1971, she confided to a diary—to become a book, *Bella*, edited by Mel Ziegler—that she knew far too little about procedure in the House. Not only was she finding the rules and regulations cumbersome and complicated, but when she learned them, it was another matter to learn how to use them.

Bella Abzug took the news that all the precedents to House Rules and Regulations had not been published since 1936 with characteristic resentment.

The problem was that Parliamentarian Lew Deschler carried all of his knowledge *locked safely inside his own head!*

"He's been ordered to publish them," Bella wrote about Deschler, "but no one knows when that will happen."

Determined to become an expert in procedure in her own right, Representative Abzug decried the time it would take.

"You've got to be creative, experienced, and know how to use the Library to ferret out what you need," wrote Bella. "What this requires is a good, solid, dependable staff."

If Bella Abzug required assistance in research, one can well imagine that at least 400 other House members are in the same position. Experienced research aides are at a premium on Capitol Hill, in the 50 state capitols, and within every city and county government.

How does one begin? Are researchers born or made?

One of our "anonymous sources" told us that a good researcher must first know where to turn for information. He pointed in the direction of *The Library*, as Bella Abzug had indicated.

"There," he said, "is all the data and information a researcher can possibly use. Regardless of demands, deadlines, how far out, how abstract or obtuse his questions, the best resource is *The Library*."

The Library is, if you haven't already guessed, the Library of Congress.

You can't miss the Library when you're on The Hill. Just east of the Capitol and neighbor to the south of the Supreme Court Building, the Library is within a few minutes walk through parklike grounds from the Senate Office Buildings, and the Rayburn, Cannon, and Longworth Office Buildings.

The building, designed by John L. Smithmeyer in 1872, was finished in 1897 at a cost of $7 million. An Annex was added for $9 million in 1939, and a second Annex, the James Madison Memorial Building, costing $90 million plus, was opened in 1975.

The quarter-century from concept to completion of the original building was typical of the careless attitude of the nineteenth century Congress toward this national treasure, called by James Truslow Adams in his book, *The Epic of America*, "a symbol of what democracy can accomplish" in its search for truth.

A massive building of magnificent architecture, the Library of Congress is a vast pile of Concord (New Hampshire) white granite. Its dome of muted colored glass panes ascends 195 feet, smaller—out of respect—than the Capitol, yet giving up nothing in majesty in its Italian Renaissance styling. Its walls rise to the height of a seven-story building, but encase only three high-ceilinged floors within.

The magnitude of the Main Reading Room has impelled our source to admit that the first few times he had visited this 125-foot high, hushed edifice, he was so awed as to nearly forget the reason for his being there.

Lucy Salamanca, in her excellent definitive book on the Library, *Fortress of Freedom*, describes the scene:

> Within this noble building, the Main Reading Room is the central feature, its marble pilasters rising, tier on tier, to its beautifully decorated and lofty dome, through the softly colored glass panes of which shafts of light stream downward upon absorbed figures bent over mahogany desks for reading or study.

Floors, stairs, and walls throughout are of marble from Algeria, Sienna (Italy), and Tennessee.

Off each marble-pillared section of the octagonal, almost

round, Reading Room are three-tiered alcoves, in which are stacks of over 25,000 volumes for quick reference by researchers.

The center of the Reading Room is taken over by a raised dais, at which sit head librarians who control the distributing desk. This desk is the terminal for a pneumatic tube system, through which books may be shuttled underground to the Capitol. A major indication of the efficiency that could be expected from the "new" library, the tube was demonstrated the week before the building was opened in November, 1897. Requested books were delivered via tube within a matter of minutes, without prearrangement or forewarning. This success was due in main to the catalog set up by Melvil Dewey, originator of the Dewey Decimal System and universally recognized as the "father" of America's public libraries.

Forming a ring around the dais, at a slightly lower level, is a circular desk where other librarians fill requests for materials. Librarians circulate around the huge room, ready to be of service to readers and researchers.

Reading desks form concentric circles around the room, their symmetry broken by islands of file drawers, which in turn make arcing lines that form parts of circles.

The 25,000 books within the Reading Room alcoves are but a scoop of whipped cream on the top of a fantastic cake.

From its beginnings in 1784 when the New York Society made its 5,000 volume library available to the Continental Congress, through the decade between 1790-1800 when the federal government convened the First Congress and moved to Philadelphia where it had access to the Library Company of America's 7,700 volumes, the new American government had no library of its own.

When the federal offices moved to Washington in 1800, $5,000 was appropriated to buy 740 books, which were placed unclassified in an empty room in the unfinished Capitol.

From this modest beginning has come the world's most complete library resource, with possessions numbering 60 million items, including:

30 million manuscript pieces
15 million books and pamphlets
3 million maps
3 million volumes and pieces of music
3 million photographic items (negatives, slides, prints)
2 million talking books for the blind
1 million Braille-character books for the blind
3 million miscellaneous items

The Library's collection of incunabula (books published before 1500) is the largest in the world. Foreign languages —particularly Russian, Chinese, and Japanese, with collections largest outside their own national spheres—are the best organized in existence.

The influence of the Library is felt wherever serious research occurs. In whatever field one seeks facts, there is always one ultimate source: the Library of Congress.

Melvil Dewey's dream was to service libraries all over the world from one central catalog system. Since Dewey's time, the National Union Catalog has come into use, a multivolumed index of published books that shows the holdings of nearly 700 large libraries in the United States.

A National Union Catalog can be found in almost all city and state libraries, and in the country's major universities and colleges.

It takes an expert to know how to find items within these catalogs. Professional librarians are available in all libraries to assist the serious researcher. It is a wise researcher who know the librarians by name.

Writer's Digest, a monthly magazine that is a forum for established as well as beginning writers, advised the researcher in their June '75 issue:

You learn about one thing quickly when you begin serious research. The people in the information biz know a thousand times more than you do. And they like you anyway.

Pointing out the elementary necessity of owning a library card, *WD* suggested that one also have at least one friend at the information desk. "And maybe a passing familiarity with some of the references there," they added.

R. R. Bowker Company, for instance, publishes an omnibus volume titled *The Reader's Adviser*; Bowker also goes into personal details about politicians and their families in *Who's Who in American Politics*. These two books are usually found in local libraries.

The Advance Locator, on the other hand, is a little more difficult to "locate." This continuing publication, by the Congressional Staff Directory (CSD), carries often changing congressional committee assignments and names staff assistants. If the *Locator* is not available in your municipal library, universities and larger colleges subscribe, as do state libraries.

The Congressional Quarterly, another subscription publication, has a weekly series of looseleaf 8 x 10 pamphlets, which when bound present an imposing annual compilation of the activities in Congress. Very little gets by the sharp editorial eyes of the CQ staff, and therefore CQ is accepted within research circles as a bible of sorts. Most leading municipal, state, and college libraries are subscribers.

Gale Research, a large Detroit-based organization, publishes an *Encyclopedia of Government Advisory Organizations*. These are hundreds of *ad hoc* panels made up of interested activist citizens promoting legislation on causes from antipornography to zero population growth.

As the researcher becomes more at home "among the stacks"—and better known among the librarians—other sources will be brought to his or her attention.

The Library of Congress offers the Congressional Research

Service (CRS), known as the Legislative Reference Service before the Legislative Reorganization Act of October 26, 1970.

The CRS serves as "honest brokers" of information, according to Charles A. Goodrum, Coordinator of Research, and in that position it aims toward a high degree of objectivity. Goodrum, well aware of the tremendous amount of information (and misinformation) that floods a congressman's office on a given subject, contends "the congressman doesn't need more advice. He needs someone who is detached, who has no axe to grind."

An increasing amount of legislation is generated by the executive branch, which apparently has no limits to its research facilities. To counterbalance this influence, the lawmakers try to bolster their own staffs and raise their own limitations. As an adjunct, they rely heavily on the CRS.

The CRS, however, has its own confines: It has no power of subpoena, and must limit its sources of information to whatever is already in the public domain.

"The Service does not and should not recommend courses of action," reads a 1970 printed release from CRS. "It endeavors to identify such choices, and to the best of its ability attempts to state the apparent strengths and weaknesses of the alternatives—but it must be the legislator who makes the decisions."

Some state legislatures have reference and research services that parallel those of CRS on a state level. These facilities are available to research staffs on a community level as well. They are usually housed within the state capitol complex, either within the Capitol itself, or in a nearby state library building.

The California Administrative Legislative Reference service (ALR) is found in the state library and courts building just west of the Capitol.

Under the direction of Mrs. Ethel S. Crockett, State Librarian, and Mrs. Irene Stone, ALR Supervising Librarian, the library has approximately 834,000 books and bound periodicals, 3,600 currently received magazines, 200 newspapers, 2¼ million government publications, and a separate law collection of 154,000 volumes.

As well as providing quick answers to who's who questions, and current addresses and telephone numbers, ALR staff members utilize the entire collection in preparing relevant materials on any subject. They also help with research, and will prepare bibliographies. Librarians scan more than 700 magazines monthly for articles of topical interest to bibliographers. They keep a file of clippings from leading newspapers, and have a complete library of state legislative bills from the current session, with access to copies of federal bills in the law section.

Research can be one phase in a career in elective government or could well become a career in itself. However, one must not necessarily become hung up on dusty book shelves and countless lonely hours among the archives to achieve a goal in politics. What is most important is to recognize the need for clear, concise, objective research in the policy-making process, and in the writing of good legislation.

Moreover, as our anonymous source told us, "Research is great fun. It's like reading history, and being a part of it at the same time. To know that information you have uncovered will be used in passing much needed legislation, and to read that section of the bill in which your words have been ascribed, is a feeling only those who have experienced can understand."

For you to do now:
Research on your own but with the help of your local librarian, one subject that is causing heated debate among your local citizenry and your elected representatives.
Remember: *Be objective!*

Chapter
7. THE DUTIES OF THE EXECUTIVE SECRETARY

If the researcher is the least noticeable of all aides in an elected official's office, the executive secretary has the most diversified and demanding position.

As do researchers, executive secretaries share common characteristics, whether they are working in the office of a small town mayor, a state legislator, a congressman, or a president.

First, the executive secretary in an elective office is usually a woman.

Second, she is a woman set apart in skills, personality, and appearance.

She must be a fast and accurate typist, although her duties may only include typing as a sometime chore.

She must be a combination Girl Friday, diplomat, discreet confidante, and knowledgeable politician.

She must be able to take flawless dictation, be an excellent speller, a hard-worker, and highly motivated.

She must be extremely tactful, with a pleasing telephone voice.

She must be a self-starter who is not a clockwatcher; she must be willing to work long hours to match those of her superior.

She must be neat, clean, polite, businesslike, interested, and interesting.

And she may be called upon to be a tourist guide, a dinner hostess, a babysitter, or a chef at a moment's notice.

If she is all of these, and more, she may command a salary upwards of $40,000.

The term "executive secretary" itself may be a misnomer. For the secretary—be she *private, personal,* or *executive*—carries many responsibilities in elective government.

In a "one woman" county supervisor's office, she may do all the accepted secretarial jobs, plus the duties found only in the office of elected politicians. These may include visiting with and assisting constituents seeking redress of grievances (casework); writing letters of condolence to the bereaved or congratulations to a local winner; researching taxation matters; preparing press releases and rough-drafting speeches; and preparing visual-aids for presentation at public hearings. She may also double as a receptionist and an information bureau.

Take the case of Dorothy C. O'Brien, executive secretary in the Washington, D.C., office of Representative Robert L. Leggett, a Democrat from California's 4th District.

"My duties in Mr. Leggett's office include handling much of his personal dictation, office accounts, seeing to it that the office runs smoothly and that correspondence from constituents is handled in timely fashion," Mrs. O'Brien told us. "On occasion when the congressman is tied up on the floor or unable to do so, I take constituents to lunch or dinner and see to their needs when in Washington."

A staff of three experienced secretaries helps Mrs. O'Brien with constituent mail. They take dictation from the member, from administrative assistant Owen Chaffee, or from other staff members and caseworkers who make up the average House office.

A member of the House of Representatives also has one or more district offices to serve the constituency. Mr. Leggett's main district office is in Vallejo, California, under the management of James Coakley, his district representative. To adequately service the far-flung 4th District, Coakley also oversees offices in the Federal and Courts Building on Capitol Mall in downtown Sacramento, and field offices in North Highlands and Del Paso Heights, north of Sacramento.

The Sacramento office is in the capable hands of Mrs. Virginia Harper, a slender, pleasant woman in her middle years, who as secretary does the composite job of staff assistant and administrative aide. At the same time she is a genuinely helpful caseworker.

In all congressional district and field offices, the heavy burden of constituent problems is carried by secretaries like Mrs. Harper.

"For example," she told us, "Social Security disability cases. Between the time the worker retires on disability, and waits the necessary six months for his eligibility, and then waits another three or four months for his first check to appear, he may think his case has hit a snag. Well, we can't bother the congressman with every case like that. So we call on a tie-line the right social security office in Birmingham, Alabama. This sometimes facilitates solving the problem."

Virginia Harper hesitated a moment.

"But not always," she smiled. "We're not miracle workers."

Cecilia Ward is executive secretary to California Assemblyman Victor Calvo, a freshman lawmaker from the 21st (Mountain View) District.

This is the fourth assembly office she has been in charge of since 1969.

"The duties of the executive secretary in state government depend a great deal on the wishes of the member," Mrs. Ward confided to us in the comparatively small office of her newest *boss*. "The member is king or queen—whichever the case may be."

Pressed for some illustrations of her job, Cecilia Ward thought for a moment, then said, "Primarily the job of the executive secretary is to be sure the member is properly advised as to his legislation and the legislation of his colleagues." She proceeded with an example:

I have a system that I devised where I keep track of all the legislation that has been introduced in that session, by number, author, date, how my member has voted in committee, what the vote was. Previously I have noted all the letters and phone calls that have come in on the bill, how many people have protested it—"I disagree with the bill Assemblyman Whoozit is pushing on birth control"—how many are for it.

I have noted any commitments my member has made pro or con the bill. These I put into the book along with other information. A daily file is distributed from the Rules Committee to members when they go into a voting session. I cross-check this daily file with the information I have compiled in my book, and I pass it all on to my member. I tell him how many have contacted the office, remind him how he has voted, what his commitments are, his reasons for being for or against. This way, he has a complete record at hand, and can concentrate on other matters. I don't believe in handing him a stack of papers and letters just before he goes into a voting session.

Reminded that this seemed to be the work of a legislative assistant rather than a secretary, Cecilia Ward laughed.

"Yes, in a way I am a legislative assistant as well as executive secretry." Suddenly serious, she added, "There is no guide book distributed by the Rules Committee, which is the committee that signs our pay vouchers, to tell a secretary just what her duties are. Each office is handled differently. I do it this way because I think it's the best way."

With no rules to follow, is there a training period?

"No. And there should be a training period, a seminar-type period in which the executive secretary would be shown exactly what is expected of her."

Mrs. Ward went on to tell of years past, when all the secretaries came from a pool, and where the person in charge of the pool handled that training phase.

"It was very efficient," she said. "But that was before the members had such huge offices and staff, so much leeway over hiring. I think there is less efficiency now."

It is particularly difficult for a new member to acquire an efficient secretarial staff, because he or she is without the necessary power (including caucus power) that comes with seniority, according to Cecilia Ward. As the member receives committee chairmanship and recognition in party caucus, his or her office size and budget goes up proportionately with the amount of "clout."

"A new member is entitled to only two secretaries in his capitol office, and one full-time working with one part-time secretary in his district office," Mrs. Ward said. "We do our best under the conditions as they are."

Secretaries of elected officials are usually in the civil service "exempt" category, and those in the California capitol are no different.

It may be more difficult than ever for freshman assemblymen and senators in California to find experienced, efficient executive secretaries. The chief of the Assembly Rules Committee's administrative office, Frederick Taugher, announced early in 1975 that secretaries of defeated members would be out of a job if they hadn't found a new lawmaker to work for within ninety days of the opening of the legislative year, February 1.

The secretarial pool, as mentioned by Cecilia Ward, would be held to a bare minimum; "bump" privileges would prevail.

Bumping means that if a secretary might stand a chance of layoff, she could insist on skills-testing, and if superior, she could bump those ahead of her on the waiting list who were less accomplished to a lower position, or bump them completely out of the employment picture.

"Your job as a legislative secretary depends on the vote-ability of your member," Cecilia Ward stated, realistically summing up her job security.

One way to reach the executive secretary position and keep it, at the same time ensuring your member's longevity in office, is through the campaign trail.

Some secretaries take to this gambit with pleasure and enthusiasm, while others do not care for campaigning at all.

"I don't like campaign work," Cecilia Ward told us, "although I know a lot of secretaries come from the districts, because they've been good campaign workers. Not that a campaign worker can't be a good secretary, but I'm against hiring someone to be a secretary just because she's been a good campaign worker. I realize that campaign work is a springboard to employment, but I don't think that's a good reason to hire somebody."

Democrat Bella Abzug from New York's 20th District seemed to concur in this thought when she wrote in *Bella*, "The campaign thing is totally different from running an office, which demands exactness and coordination. . . ."

However, campaign work helped Virginia Harper be considered for her important post in Sacramento.

"This is my first political job," she told us. "I worked all my life as a secretary, and happened to be on leave from my position as secretary-administrative aide at the University of California's Davis campus. Mr. Leggett knew me from my activity in volunteer politics. He knew I knew the big seven-county district, that I knew lots of people in it. He knew I could run an office. So my political experience did have something to do with my getting the job. Plus, of course, my secretarial experience."

Mrs. Harper added a thought about loyalty.

"It has to be someone who is loyal to the congressman who will make the best secretary. He knew I was loyal because I'd been working not only in his campaign, but in campaigns of other Democratic candidates."

Pausing for a moment, Mrs. Harper quickly amended, "I will always help my boss when election time comes around. But this is not a campaign office. This office is for the constituents. The campaign can come beyond these doors, but not really. This is still the constituents' office, for casework."

Dorothy O'Brien came to Washington from Michigan in 1959 when Senator Philip A. Hart was elected. She worked on the senator's staff for two years, handling some of his correspondence, and constituents' requests, along with postal department and service academy matters.

When John F. Kennedy decided to run for the presidency, she became involved in the civil rights platform—Senator Hart "more or less wrote the views on this issue along with several civil rights activists," according to Mrs. O'Brien.

After Kennedy was elected, Dorothy O'Brien accompanied him to the White House where she worked in the presidential appointments section under Kenneth O'Donnell for about a year, helping process the thousands of applications for assignments in the "New Frontier."

"I found the work exciting in the White House," Mrs. O'Brien admitted, "but the hours were too much for me since I had a family. I left and did several part time jobs before I joined the staff of Congressman Leggett when he was first elected. I've been with him ever since."

What background and prerequisites are necessary to successfully apply for one of these positions?

"Most of what I learned was learned while on the job," Dorothy O'Brien said. "I did not go to college. I am a graduate of a business school in Detroit, Michigan. But I certainly have learned the game of politics while on the job, and consider myself quite knowledgeable, if I do say so."

Edna M. McLellan was an airline stewardess before she went to work for Gladys N. Spellman as a clerk-typist in Prince Georges County, Maryland, at $1.75 per hour. Today Mrs. McLellan is executive assistant in Representative Spellman's D.C. office at $20,000 per year. Mrs. McLellan had

also worked for others in local government before leaving
for the greener pastures on The Hill, most notably County
Councilman Francis B. Francois, a political ally of Congress-
woman Spellman. This unofficial liaison between federal
and local government is a much desired and sought after
situation, and serves as a natural step up the employment
ladder for anyone lucky enough or wise enough to place
oneself into position.

"The cream of the crop *is* in Washington," Virginia Harper
emphasized during our visit to Representative Leggett's
Sacramento office. "And that's where the pay is."

Can one go directly to Capitol Hill and hope to find immediate employment?

"There is a good personnel office that helps," Mrs. Harper
answered our question. "A pool through which the House
of Representatives hires. It is called the Office of Placement
and Office Management. Most certainly they'd have to buck
a waiting list, but if I were a young person that's where I'd
want to go. It seems so much more exciting to be at the seat
of the action, where the laws are made. . . ."

(Mrs. Harper was interrupted by the telephone—an opposition call about the Vietnam evacuees. Mrs. Harper noted
it on a pad, and then continued her line of thought.)

"They'd have to be very good at what they do," she said.
"If they are secretary-stenos, they'd have to be excellent at
that. It's not all that easy back in Washington. But if they
do get in, it's much more exciting to work on The Hill, and
in the legislature back there in the House or in the Senate."

Virginia Harper's position was undoubtedly enhanced by
her long experience as a secretary, but it is unquestionable
that her flair for the political end of her office is useful.

"It sounds like a do-gooder," she said about her newly
found responsibility as district secretary, "but I'm really delighted to do casework, and to work for the congressman
in this way. I think it's a privilege to help people who need
it."

The telephone rang again, for at least the tenth time since our visit to Congressman Leggett's office began. We looked out the fourth floor window at the view of Capitol Mall and tried not to eavesdrop.

"That was a woman trying to get information on her grandfather's 1872 naturalization papers," Virginia Harper explained. "She has written to the bureaucracy in Washington without success. She will send us the information we need, and we will follow up through the Bureau of Archives." Mrs. Harper seemed confident that the caller's problems were about to be solved.

Going back to the trend of our conversation, we wondered what were the strongest credentials necessary for the potential employee in an elected official's office.

"In my mind," Virginia Harper answered, "if I were a congressman, I'd want resource people more than I'd want anybody to run the office. Because you don't run it the way you'd run a business. You've got too many problems each day. Each day is a brand new day. You just don't do your same bookkeeping as you did the day before. Or the same letters. Each letter is entirely different. Each problem."

When asked which attributes she thought most valuable for a young person to become not only a good resource person, but a good secretary, or general staff person, she hesitated not at all.

"Good journalists. People who can really write. Those are the people who are needed. Researchers. Lots of them double as speechwriters in all legislators' offices. That doesn't mean the congressman is going to take that speech. But he's going to get an idea from that speech, and use it when he writes his own."

This brought to mind Mayor Richard Marriott's emphatic pronouncement: *Learn how to use the language.*

The secretary who is able to make corrections in written English grammar and possesses basic reading and writing skills will be more successful in a career choice than one who lacks them.

The choice of secretarial school often is the difference between struggling for employment and immediate acceptance.

"Our training not only includes the mechanical skills required of a secretary," we were told by Edna B. Groves, a placement director in the large Heald Business College, northern California chain. "We are especially proud of our Business English program, which smooths out the rough spots in our students' language, reading, and writing background."

Mrs. Elta Langbehn, instructor in Business English and Business Communication at Heald's Sacramento college, finds the problems brought to her classes by students fresh from high school to be "tremendous."

"Although there has been improvement recently," she admits, "since junior high and high school teachers have become aware of the reading and writing shortcomings."

Heald's courses include 120 clock-hours of English grammar and 60 clock-hours for Communication, plus "1½ to 2 hours per subject daily in outside work," according to Mrs. Langbehn.

The methodology used at Heald's in its English and Communication classes carries over into other areas of curricula, most specifically in dictation and transcription.

"It is here that we find out if the student has achieved superiority," says Mrs. Langbehn.

Why should a student learn better English, punctuation, and communication in a business college, when the lessons so obviously haven't been learned before?

"Perhaps it's that the student has made a dollar investment, and to have the investment pay must make the extra effort to learn," Mrs. Langbehn said.

Whether or not the student makes the most of his or her education, be it tuition-free public high school or dollar-invested business college, the "something extra" to which we alluded earlier is most important as a catalyst to obtaining one of these positions.

Cecilia Ward illustrated that indefinable something early in her career when she was in an executive secretarial position within the Fresno, California, school administration.

"I worked for the administrators, curriculum officer, superintendent, consultants," she recalled, "and they tried to think of a title for me because, in effect, I created my own job. Beginning as a secretary to the curriculum coordinator, I manufactured another job so that I then became manager of that department. I coordinated all the work for twelve consultants in secondary education curricula, as well as elementary education. In addition, I had four secretaries working for me whose work I coordinated."

Mrs. Ward's eyes sparkled as she related her story.

"Because I had no title, and wasn't an educator—I had one year of high school typing, one semester of shorthand, a little more typing and shorthand in college—it sometimes became necessary for me to be quite forceful."

We smiled as Cecilia Ward, a petite redheaded woman, described herself.

"I was known, and labeled, as the most charmingly obnoxious person in the district," she laughed.

"If you're the type that wants to get something done," Cecilia Ward proclaimed, "and you've got something to offer, it is very hard as a secretary to have the prestige that will make possible the thing you want done. The principals and vice-principals didn't like it at all for this little redheaded secretary to tell them what to do."

It sometimes takes, as Cecilia Ward demonstrated, *executive presence* to become an executive secretary.

For you to do now:
You will always need typing and shorthand skills; practice them now.
Brush up on your grammar, spelling, and handwriting.

Chapter
8. THE MANY CHORES OF GENERAL STAFF

Another round in the game of "shared distinctions":

A young, $80 per week secretary, civil-service-exempt, the lone employee in a small town mayor's office; an unpaid volunteer campaign "gopher"—meaning "go for"—person; a governor's $27,500 per year press aide; a White House executive assistant; a congressional liaison consultant working out of the Department of Health, Education and Welfare ($40,000 per year).

What do they have in common?

They are the backbone of government as we know it in the United States.

They are the staff, "the selected by the elected."

Staff is such a general term, and encompasses such a wide scope of activities in government, that books have been written on the occupation of staff personnel.

Conversely, little is included in the literature predating the Legislative Reorganization Act of 1946.

Gladys M. Kammerer wrote one of the first studies on congressional staffing for *The American Political Science Review* (December, 1951) as an offshoot from her own academic studies beginning in 1948.

Prior to 1946, Kammerer noted,

The point had been made repeatedly by critics within and outside the Congress that its standing committees must be equipped with first-rate professional staffs if they are to make intelligent legislative decisions on the complex and technical problems presented to the legislators for solution. Reliance upon executive branch research studies . . . was held by many to be fraught with the danger of injecting special pleading and biases for the increasing number of administration-sponsored bills. For Congress to function as a coequal partner with the executive in the legislative process, these critics deemed it essential that Congress empower itself to obtain its own independent staff services and that it pay adequately for them.

Before 1946, individual members of Congress and the standing committees were more or less dependent on the executive branch and its agencies for facts and expert interpretation. Even after the Act became law, problems with the quality of appointments, the lack of any systematic personnel arrangements, and questions of tenure added up to a giant headache in committee circles.

Today, however, staffing has become a professional career assignment in federal, state, and local government. The lack of "steady job" tenure has not affected the direction of those who would pursue the position of trained and experienced staff personnel.

Excluding the *housekeeping* staff from our study and centering on the *specialist* and *professional* staff better suits our purposes. The housekeeping staff performs clerical, secretarial, and relatively routine service tasks; the research, bill-drafting, investigating, and politicial staff members are more dependent on the voteability of the "patron" and the decisions of the electorate.

In most states, the legislator has no staff assistance. However, some staff services available to legislators in thirty-eight states for research purposes is under the control of a research council staff director.

Under these conditions, according to Jewell and Patterson in *The Legislative Process in the United States,*

> The policy position of the research staff and its general effectiveness are associated with the personality and capacities of the Director. He may develop a viable and effective staff, intimately involved in the legislative policy-making process; or he may, by ineptness or incapacity, wreck the research operation.

For this reason, larger and more sophisticated states such as New York and California have put staff personnel organizing into the hands of the various legislative members.

In some states, including Kentucky, the research staff is actually a part of the executive branch. Illinois, on the other hand, runs its research staffing through a legislative council, which provides accurate information to individual legislators, and goes so far as to assist in speech material and preparing both pro and con arguments on bills.

The Kansas legislative council takes part in the legislative process and makes policy recommendations.

California has majority and minority consultant services, which include research analysts and legislative specialists, as well as aides for individual legislators.

Perhaps more than any other state, California staffing most accurately parallels the congressional and executive branch staffing as found in Washington and congressional district offices.

The Citizens Conference on State Legislatures has awarded the California legislature the accolade, "outstanding State legislative body in the nation," primarily because of staff capabilities in assisting the members of the assembly and senate in the performance of their duties.

Another similarity with Washington staffing is found in Sacramento: unwritten rules following closely—but not too closely—the governmental code. Unmentionable salaries, discovered through unquotable sources. Party caucus power leading to committee power leading to staffing power. Political manipulation through staff power. Individual preferences of legislators in selecting staff—staunch campaign worker, old campus ties, friend-of-a-friend—sometimes surpassing other qualities.

And, until recently, the coincidence of marriage and birth —wife, son, brother-in-law, nephew—was acceptable as a prerequisite in staff hiring, or "clerk hire" as staffing has been called down the years.

All this has transpired within the benign purview of the party in power in the state legislatures, the United States Senate Rules Committee, or the Committee on House Administration.

Not that the spoils system still holds forth in our national capitol or in our state houses, as it did in the 1800s. It doesn't. But patronage is not dead, not in Washington, not in your own state capitol, and not in your city hall. It is under the discreet control of ethics committees, and a more logical approach by the policymakers themselves.

What quality makes a person a good prospective aide then, regardless of patronage?

As Virginia Harper said, "It has to be someone the congressman can be sure will be loyal to him."

Dorothy O'Brien told us another factor: "I would say that your political views would have to coincide with those of your boss or you would be in conflict with yourself on the issues. For instance, I cannot imagine myself working for a conservative, as we would not agree on anything."

Cecilia Ward, who has worked for both Democrats and Republicans, says, "It is good to have the same philosophy as your boss. But I don't think it's good to agree on everything. It's a good *devil's advocate* for him to have someone close to him who will give him feedback from another viewpoint."

Mrs. Ward doesn't think it would be a workable situation if one were a staunch conservative and the other a rebellious radical, however.

"Not if either one cared a great deal about either side," she says, adding quickly, "I must say, though, that some offices are kind of dead, in-bred, without a spark, because all the thinking is in such close agreement."

New York Representative Bella Abzug had considerable difficulty lining up her first staff.

"I spent the last two months interviewing dozens of people for various jobs I had to fill in my Washington office," she wrote in *Bella*. "An administrative assistant, a legislative assistant, a caseworker, a receptionist, a personal secretary and scheduler, people to answer letters."

Some of the applicants had communicated their desire to work for Mrs. Abzug after her first successful campaign. Some names came from the House Democratic Study Group, an organization that, among its services, finds places for liberal congressional aides.

Others who had worked for defeated congressmen were making the rounds of the Senate and House office buildings seeking employment.

With all these sources, Bella Abzug still had difficulty finding the right personnel.

"I knew exactly what I was looking for," she wrote. "People experienced on The Hill who also were activists and radicals. But as you can imagine, people with that combination of attributes are not readily available, if they exist at all."

We were curious about Mrs. Abzug's current staffing problems, or lack of them, now that she had some years to put her offices in good working order. This is her answer:

I have a very competent hard-working staff in Washington and New York. The total is 18, although recently we got extra allowances to hire two additional people. The perennial problem for many members of Congress, including myself, is staff turnover in Washington. My New York staff has been with me, most of them, since the beginning. The workload in Washington is staggering and the pay comparatively low, so that staff members, willing as they may be, find the pace and volume of work exhausting and they last a year or two, then use their experience to get easier, higher-paying jobs. I understand why this happens, only unfortunately I don't think the general public understands the enormous amount of work involved in running a *conscientious* and responsive Congressional office.

The emphasis on conscientious is Bella Abzug's. She is noted in her district as being an extremely responsive and innovative representative, one who works as hard or harder than any of her colleagues.

Full-time congressional staff salaries begin at $8,000, and go upwards of $20,000 as experience and responsibilities increase.

Why are large staffs necessary at all?

This, of course, is the question asked by many overloaded taxpayers, and the answer doesn't come easily unless one sees government in action, not only on the federal level, but in every state capitol and municipality from coast to coast.

The answer is three-faceted:

> Size of population
> Demands of the electorate for services
> Numbers of mandated programs

When George Washington took office, one part-time clerk was all the staff necessary to help run the executive branch. The first Congress had only one program: to write a Constitution. One secretary-clerk was on hand; the framers did all of the writing.

The Constitution itself was made necessary by the inability of the states to get along among themselves.

Jethro K. Lieberman wrote in his book, *Understanding Our Constitution:*

> Some legislatures openly passed laws in violation of provisions contained in their State constitutions, declaring jury trials invalid, taking property, sentencing men to death without a trial, destroying newspapers, reversing judgments of courts, and behaving often as arrogantly as the king who had been overthrown.

Congress, before the Constitution, was unable to enforce laws under the loosely drawn Articles of Federation covering such necessities as revenues, regulation of commerce, and payment of the $42 million war debt.

The five basic principles of the Constitution—federalism, separation of powers, checks and balances, rule by majority, and unalienable rights—have not been taken lightly by Congress in the first two centuries of life under its protection.

To properly govern through the Constitution, Congress needed more and more assistance as the nation grew. Today it presents and studies in depth between 20,000 and 25,000 bills and resolutions in each two-year session.

The power of the executive branch grew apace.

In our adversary method of balancing executive proposals and congressional restraints (and vice versa), sufficient resources are essential so that each side has the knowledge and background to manage with diligence all phases of a given problem.

Here is where competent staffing is important.

Often students of law and economics will spend a year or two in state government or in Washington for the experience to be gained; many times they leave with the feeling of rewarding accomplishment, and find that they would like to return to the policymaking arena.

One of these individuals is Stewart W. (Sandy) Kemp, Boston lawyer and part-time teacher of economics in Cambridge.

"Somewhat paradoxically perhaps," Sandy told us, "I was impressed during my Washington experience both by how much and by how little one person could accomplish. How much when judged realistically in terms of the complexity and varied constituencies surrounding any important issue, and how little when compared to the idealistic fervor of a crusader determined to change the world."

Sandy spent a year on the staff of a presidential commission studying the draft and the volunteer army (1969-70), followed by a year as director of the National Council of Repeal the Draft. This experience gave him two different perspectives on the political process.

As a staff member of the commission—his undergraduate thesis had been on the subject—Kemp was responsible for researching certain aspects of the issue and writing several chapters of the final report.

"On one level," he recalled, "the process was quite similar to my academic work, but the determination of the final recommendations was a classically political process, involving compromise among differing points of view and interests."

Then Sandy Kemp made a statement that underlines the importance of staff intelligence and integrity:

Despite their total absence of official authority, it was remarkable to see the extent to which members of the staff—through their superior understanding of the issue, control of information, and the actual drafting of the report—determined the substance as well as the form of the final recommendations.

Kemp's primary role on the council was as a lobbyist and organizer, "the former to educate on the merits of the issue and the latter to demonstrate to legislators the extent of public concern" concerning draft repeal.

"My own work was much more active than it had been with the commission," Sandy said, "as I arranged numerous meetings with members of Congress and their staffs and did a fair amount of media work and public speaking."

Coordinating speakers for the now-famous April 24 Capitol rally; soliciting contributions from the public—"our only source of support"; garnering senatorial votes after good discussions with a legislative assistant; seeing a national newspaper or magazine article come to life following a discussion with its author—these are the satisfying aspects of a job that stay with a person.

In retrospect, Sandy has difficulty in assessing the effectiveness of the work of the commission.

"On the one hand, the draft authority was not extended, but on the other, it might have ended anyway. In view of the educational void which our lobbying efforts filled, and the feedback we received from the people we dealt with, I'm sure we played a significant role."

On a personal level, however, Sandy Kemp has no doubts.

"The excitement and sense of purpose and accomplishment made the experience the most rewarding work that I've ever undertaken."

It is not betraying a confidence to say that Kemp may soon return to the political scene. He told us, "The sense of immediate effectiveness can be lacking in day-to-day law practice, both because of the lengthy character of legal proceedings and the necessity of complying with existing requirements rather than creating new policy."

Where is the action? Among the policymakers!

"Bright, hard-working, and ambitious, ranging in age from

their late 20's to their early 30's, they have leap-frogged over the seniority system of civil service to be near power and often have had a hand in wielding it."

This is the way Connecticut Walker described the "Young Men at the Top in Washington" for *Parade* Magazine (June 1, 1975).

Walker gave a rundown on a few of the "names" that are becoming known outside The Hill and the White House.

William Taft, ex-aide to consumer advocate, Ralph Nader, has been assistant to former Health, Education and Welfare Secretary Caspar Weinberger. Taft's salary, at age 29, is $36,000 per year.

Rick Tropp, 27, special counsel to the Presidential Clemency Board; Jerry Bremer, 33-year-old executive assistant to Secretary of State Henry Kissinger; John Reed, executive assistant to former Secretary of Labor John T. Dunlop; Richard Cheney, 34, top aide to Donald Rumsfeld, former presidential chief of staff. All of these young men get salaries up to $40,000 per year.

These staff members earn their wages. Their duties range from coordinating White House staff operations to expediting presidential paperwork; they review and study all issues that come into the scope of each one's principal; they act as liaison between agency heads and secretaries; they are speech writers, policy consultants, legislative researchers.

Long, long hours and extensive travel are part of the game, and for these factors alone youth and stamina are assets.

Jerry Bremer, for example, traveled so many miles and was gone from home so much working for and with Secretary Kissinger, that "my two-year-old daughter hardly knew who I was." Bremer estimates he covered a quarter of a million miles in 1974, and Kissinger is noted for his fourteen hour days. Bremer, as any other efficient aide would do, usually worked two hours more.

Too often the House and Senate do not have the resources to balance the powerful staffing entity on the executive end of Pennsylvania Avenue.

That staffing in the Senate might be increased to meet the demands for more oversight responsibility over abuses of power by the executive, Democrat Mike Gravel, senator from Alaska, submitted Senate Resolution 110 on March 11, 1975.

Speaking before the Committee on Rules and Administration, Senator Gravel gave his reasons for preparing the resolution:

> As I reviewed my first Senate term and began making plans for my second, I became acutely aware that my ability to meaningfully participate in a great many issues was seriously hampered by a lack of staff. There is no question in my mind that there exists a positive correlation between the number of staff a member has and the number of issues in which he can become involved. There is also no question that the depth of a member's knowledge on a broad range of subjects depends on the amount of capable staff under his direction.

Pointing out that there are two methods by which the Senate is provided staff—the population formula, which takes into account the number of constituents a senator must serve, and committee staffing, which provides cadres of professionals to guide the Senate as a whole in major policy areas—Senator Gravel proposed a third category to ensure individual senators have expert assistance in meeting their legislative assignments.

"In talking to members about Senate Resolution 110, I have learned that many subcommittee chairmen have received no staff even after six, eight or ten years of service," Gravel told the Rules and Administration Committee. "This occurs because each committee chairman runs his committee differently . . . staffs are not allowed to expand to a size equal to their tasks."

This was particularly true in regard to subcommittees, according to Gravel.

"My amendment to the Senate rules would put some equality into our staffing procedures, enhance our oversight capability, assist the Senate in its efforts to re-establish the Congress as a truly equal branch of government. . . ."

Coauthoring S. Res. 110 with Gravel, Alan Cranston, Democratic senior senator from California, claimed that his current staff budget of $930,000 for 69 assistants—nine committee aides and 60 personal staff—is "deplorably understaffed." Fifteen additional helpers would raise his staff payroll to $1.2 million.

Too much money? Not when you consider Cranston's constituency numbers 21 million, or that he serves on five committees and is chairman of three subcommittees.

His colleague, John V. Tunney, junior senator from California, shares his views and the same number of constituents. Tunney is on nineteen subcommittees. To keep abreast of the problems engendered on these subcommittees alone requires more staff, and this does not consider the continuing problems of the electorate, according to Tunney.

Senator Gravel's resolution would add 500 new staff jobs on The Hill, at an annual cost of $16 million.

Where are these new staff members to originate?

Some will be recruited from various state legislatures, and from the larger cities such as New York, Los Angeles, Chicago, and Cleveland.

It is hoped that many staff members will come from high school and college campuses. Mike Gravel told us this in a personal letter, saying that "instructors must be thoroughly familiar with such factors as the role of purely political consideration in the governing process and the role that severe time and resource limitations play in decision making.

"Summer programs or leaves of absence for high school and college instructors must be encouraged," Senator Gravel said. "Teachers of government and political science should more readily avail themselves of congressional staff to serve as guest lecturers. Many senators and congressmen have field staffs in their districts that would be pleased to speak to classes about their tasks and many varied roles."

With teachers of government in high schools and colleges speaking from firsthand experience, and with staff assistants from local, state, and federal offices imparting their collective knowledge to classes, soon the necessity—and the role—of general staff will become better known among the electorate.

For you to do now:
With the concurrence of your instructor, invite a legislative assistant, an administrative assistant, or any member of general staff within your local, state, or congressional office to speak at a school political group meeting.

Youth involvement in campaigning. Above, with the assistance of a "staff" member, Clare Berryhill blows up balloons alongside the bus in which he and his family traveled over 60,000 miles in a successful quest for the post of California state senator. Below, the Berryhill brass ensemble, all high school students, gives off with some hot licks to draw a crowd of county fairgoers. *(R. V. D. photo)*

Gov. Edmund G. Brown, Jr., answers some questions posed by students during a stroll between the Sacramento Community Center and his capitol office.

(R. V. D. photo)

Paul Cheverton, seated, vice-president of the California Student Republican Organization, confers with Carl Davis, III, of the Claremont High School Young Republicans.

(R. V. D. photo)

Kristi Jenkins enrolls a delegate to support her candidate at the Republican Central Committee Convention. *(R. V. D. photo)*

Cecilia Ward, executive secretary. *(R. V. D. photo)*

When United States Representative Robert L. Leggett, Democrat from California's 4th District, needs home-office input, he will call assistant Ed Cheever (below) on the red phone tie line. Constituents always have a direct line to Washington through their district representative. (*R. V. D. photo*)

A dome-high view of one-half of the octagonal-shaped Main Reading Room, Library of Congress, Washington, D.C.

(Courtesy the Library of Congress)

The media at work. Above, a student reporter queries Congressman Barry Goldwater, Jr. Below, television political reporter Heidi Schulman (KNBC-Los Angeles) speaks to an unseen audience as a sound engineer checks for voice level.

(R. V. D. photo)

John McNeece, Stanford Phi Beta Kappa, at work as a legislative intern before entering Boalt Hall, University of California, Berkeley, law school. *(R. V. D. photo)*

Judi Phillips, lobbyist, confers with Assemblyman Dixon Arnett following his introduction of a proposal in support of an amendment to the U. S. Constitution establishing the initiative process and vote of confidence (recall) process at a federal level. The populist proposal was prompted by People's Lobby, by whom Ms. Phillips is employed. *(R. V. D. photo)*

Jackie Habecker, receptionist for five California governors: Earl Warren, Goodwin J. Knight, Edmund G. Brown, Sr., Ronald Reagan, and Edmund G. Brown, Jr. (*R. V. D. photo*)

Edward V. Roberts of Berkeley, a quadriplegic since he was stricken with polio as a teenager, chats with Governor Jerry Brown (Edmund G., Jr.) following his swearing-in as California Director of the Department of Rehabilitation.

(*Courtesy Sacramento BEE*)

Chapter

9. THE RESPONSIBILITIES OF LEGISLATIVE COUNSEL AND LEGISLATIVE ANALYST

Two career opportunities closely related to elective government, but untouched by party politics and policy debates, are found within the offices of the legislative counsel and the legislative analyst.

Each position, however, depends on joint resolutions of state legislatures or Congress for assignment and is civil service exempt; for these reasons we have included them in our study.

The need for legal advice in bill drafting was recognized as long ago as 1895, when the California legislature created a commission to revise and reform then-current laws. The Senate and Assembly requested that commissioners attend sessions and act as "legislative counsel or adviser, in drafting or passing upon the form of any bill or proposed bill, pending, or to be introduced before the Legislature."

In 1913, the Legislative Counsel Bureau was established by statute as a state agency to assist the legislature with bill drafting and statutory revision functions.

The first Legislative Counsel Bureau was selected by a board consisting of the governor and two members of each house of the legislature. In 1917, the position was made appointive *at the pleasure of the governor.*

In 1927, however, California law adopted the present procedure: the counsel is selected by the joint legislature.

The primary requisite is that the counsel be selected without reference to political party affiliation and solely upon the ground of fitness to perform the duties of the office. In one form or another, the legislatures of all states now have the services of counsel.

Congress is served by separate counsel for each house, Representatives and Senate.

Written into law in 1921, the Office of the Legislative Counsel was begun largely through the individual efforts of a man named Middleton Beaman.

Mr. Beaman had been sent to Congress in 1916 by the Legislative Drafting Research Fund to demonstrate the usefulness of a skilled legislative draftsman.

The Fund was an endowment of Joseph P. Chamberlain to Columbia University in 1911.

". . . the contribution of Mr. Beaman to the establishment and successful functioning of the Office of the Legislative Counsel can hardly be overemphasized," wrote Kenneth Kofmehl in *Professional Staffs of Congress.* "In fact, it might be said that the Office was an institutionalization of Mr. Beaman."

Beaman continued as House Legislative Counsel for thirty years until January 31, 1949. The assignments to staff positions under Beaman became choice goals for young lawyers, not so much for the salary ranges, but for the experience in legislative and constitutional law, and in bill drafting.

Beginning under the training designation of "law assistant," recruits to staff positions are given meticulous on-the-job preparation. Recommended by the deans of the country's leading law schools, candidates face close scrutiny while undergoing a protracted period of in-service training before acceptance.

"At every stage," said Kofmehl, "they give him advice on how to handle various tasks. . . . Nothing he prepares leaves the office without being reviewed. . . . They stress every conceivable item for which he should be on the lookout . . . they inquire if he had considered the constitutional issues involved—whether there were any or not. . . . One assistant counsel likened this review procedure to a hazing upper classmen administer to a plebe at West Point."

The result of this system has been an agency upon which both the House and Senate can depend for accuracy, keen insight into the legislative process free from political pressures, and professional confidentiality with individual lawmakers and committees alike.

The California legislative counsel serves both Assembly and Senate. The present title belongs to George H. Murphy, who was selected for the position in 1964.

The legislative counsel has no tenure of office other than that given by the assumption that, if a good job is done, the legislature will see fit to continue him or her in office. However, the entire staff is required to be appointed under the civil service system, with the exception of two exempt appointments granted the counsel by the state constitution.

One of the principal reasons for the existence of the Office of the Legislative Counsel is to advise and assist the legislature and its members and committees in the preparation of legislation. The office is frequently asked to "expert" a bill prepared under private sponsorship with a view to making technical suggestions which might improve the bill.

However, a prohibition scrupulously observed is found in Section 10210 of the Government Code, which provides that "Neither the Legislative Counsel nor any employee of the Bureau shall oppose or urge legislation."

As in Congress, the state legislative counsel and his or her staff maintain an attorney-client relationship with each member with respect to the work performed for that member. This means that, unless expressly authorized by the member, no request by the member or the fact that such a request has been made, will be discussed with any other member, any member of the press, or any other person not employed by the legislative counsel.

The services of the office are available only to members of the legislature, with limited exceptions set forth in the statutes. Therefore, when another elected constitutional office (secretary of state or lieutenant governor, for example) needs expert assistance, it is up to their staff to supply it.

It was such a need that led to Susan Sawyer's first job out of Boalt Hall, the University of California's Berkeley campus law school.

We sat in Ms. Sawyer's tiny office in the East Wing Capitol Annex, within the California lieutenant governor's suite. The area outside the office was a jumble of folding screens, portable partitions, and desks, chairs, and filing cabinets. The old Capitol West Wing, the golden dome and cupola, and the legislative chambers were undergoing earthquake-proof rebuilding.

"Since I am a lawyer," Susan Sawyer began, "I was looking for legal jobs, but I saw this one advertised."

The ad in a school publication was for a legal counsel to work in Sacramento. What Susan Sawyer didn't know was that she was to become the lieutenant governor's expert on Proposition 9, the initiative that the voters hope will carry California into a new era of political responsibility.

"Now I'm the person everyone checks with when they have a legal question." She smiled hesitantly. "I didn't study 'Prop 9' before I came here. I'm still learning.

"There are so many questions as to the legality of gifts," she continued. "For instance, a press photo, one that we thought was very good, that we'd like to have in our files. The question: Could they legally give us the picture?"

The legal implications of Prop 9 have had everyone in California elective offices spinning, and we found it interesting that even the office of the lieutenant governor was affected.

"It's very complicated," Susan Sawyer admitted. "Unfortunately a lot of the things with which we deal here are not taught in law school. There is nothing, at least where I went to school, on legislative drafting. This would be very useful. For instance, now I am drafting a code of ethics for our office. Under Prop 9, every agency has to formulate its own conflict of interest law. Beyond the conflict of interest requirements for staff, this office would like to expand, to make the office a tight ship ethically."

We inquired, now that she had spent some time in the Capitol, whether any other branch of state government might hold Susan's interest.

Susan Sawyer thought for a brief moment, then replied, "I've been pretty much impressed by the legislators here. More than I anticipated. It's broken a lot of stereotypes that I had of politicians. Yes, in the sense that you have some real access to getting bills through, the legislature might be interesting."

Then Susan told us a fascinating story.

"When I first knew I was coming here, I had a kind of fantasy about what it would be like to work in the State Capitol. I had spent a couple of days here being interviewed, and I think those days fed my fantasy. The fantasy was of *go, go, go!* All the time. You were off to this meeting, talking to some well-known senator. Then off to another meeting, talking to an assemblyman. Then discussing policy with someone in the legislative analyst's office."

Susan Sawyer shrugged pointedly.

"I think the first two weeks I was here—it was a process of becoming familiar. Reading a lot. Sitting in my office. It was just an office job, and it was very disappointing."

She smiled philosophically.

"Since then, the job has involved days like that. Not seeing people except for casual conversation. But there are days when, while not approaching my fantasy of discussing policy with the governor or something, it's a lot of fun. Because there is a lot of razzle-dazzle. Meetings all day, which never seem very much like work to me. A lot of people-contact, talking, getting information from other people on the phone. Those days are a lot of fun."

Her eyes sparkled.

"And I can see why people get into politics. Legislators are doing much more than I do, and it seems an exciting way to live."

As legislation became more complicated, government services proliferated, and billions of dollars flowed from taxpayer to local, state, and national treasuries, the need for a budget commission separate from both executive and legislative bodies became apparent.

In California during the 1930s, members of the legislature realized that the governor had large and experienced budget and audit staffs that completely overshadowed their own understanding of technical data; they decided to create a staff for this purpose.

However, it wasn't until 1951 that the legislature enacted and the governor signed into law Chapter 1667, which now provides a statutory basis for the Joint Legislative Budget Committee and the office of the legislative analyst.

With regard to the responsibilities of the Joint Legislative Budget Committee, Chapter 1667 provides that it "shall ascertain facts and make recommendations to the Legislature and to the Houses thereof concerning the State Budget, the revenues and expenditures of the State, the organization and functions of the State, its departments, subdivisions, and agencies, and such other matters as may be provided for in the Joint Rules of the Senate and the Assembly."

Among other duties, the legislative analyst makes recommendations about all the money that is taken in and paid out; assists in all legislation that affects budget or appropriations; and sees to it that all legislative committees are informed about all bills.

The analyst is also expected to propose statutory changes to effect operational economies and more effective administration, and to recommend areas and methods for research studies to be undertaken by the administration, the budget committee, or any other legislative committee.

To staff an office with this high degree of responsibility requires fifty technical and nineteen clerical positions. *Staff members are not in the civil service system.* However, the office follows the civil service practices regarding salary levels, retirement, vacations, and related benefits.

A low staff turnover has led to the development of specialists with expertise which makes it possible for them to deal with technical and policy issues on a scale with agency administrators of the highest rank.

The office of the legislative analyst boasts that its product is that of a technically trained and professionally oriented staff operating on a continuing and nonpartisan basis. Although the legislative analyst serves *at the pleasure of the committee,* the position has been filled since its inception by only two individuals.

The current legislative analyst in California, A. Alan Post, has served in this capacity since 1949.

In describing his staff, Mr. Post says, "Most staff members have graduate degrees in economics or political science. However, we do have other specialists which include three professional engineers and an architect for analysis of construction, resources, transportation and related fields; one attorney; one CPA and several with business management, accounting, and electronic data processing backgrounds."

Staff members are expected to be well versed in the legal basis, organization, activities, and workloads of each agency to which they may be assigned.

These agencies are found in nine general areas, each headed by a principal program analyst:

1. Health and Welfare
2. Revenues, Taxation and Fiscal
3. Natural Resources and Agricultural
4. Electronic Data Processing and General Service
5. Correctional and Judicial
6. Construction and Transportation
7. Expenditure Controls and Projections
8. Education
9. Higher Education

Other states are following California's lead in forming the office of legislative analyst, and in recent years municipalities have also added the office to their policymaking and taxing entities.

All are under the control of the citizen through his or her elected representative.

For you to do now:
Research your own state and local government.
Determine whether the safeguards offered by the offices of legislative counsel and legislative analyst are available to you and your family and friends—the citizens and taxpayers.

Chapter
10. HOW TO QUALIFY FOR AN INTERN PROGRAM

Perhaps the most positive way for a young American student to achieve a place in elective government—local, state, or federal—is through an *intern program.*

Internships in government are designed to allow the student various degrees of exposure to the often confusing, always exciting world of legislation, policymaking, and fiscal juggling.

Virtually unheard of before 1953, intern programs have grown to include Master's graduates, baccalaureate undergrads, and even high school students within their numbers.

While many government internships carry assignments within civil service areas, it is generally accepted that the majority owe their existence to the patronage-of-sorts offered by elected officialdom, as well as cooperating academic institutions and foundations. For the purposes of our study, we will cover as closely as possible only internships related directly to elective government.

Interns in government share all the duties of their often well-paid counterparts on administrative, legislative, and executive staff. These duties include researching technical questions, answering constituent mail, consulting with constituents, sitting in on conferences and making suggestions, assisting in bill drafting, assisting in speech drafting, performing administrative assignments for committees, and running countless errands for the boss.

Along with these assignments, the intern is expected to attend academic seminars featuring guest lecturers who explain the legislative process; learn the preparation of and discuss research papers; and join talk sessions with legislators, lobbyists, academicians, and journalists.

An internship experience has been described by Frank Logue in his monograph *Who Administers?*, written for the Ford Foundation, as a "determining factor," of equal importance with personal contact with someone in the field of government, and the availability of support funds while studying, for anyone opting for a career in government. Internships are particularly valuable to students of urban administration, according to Logue.

In California, 112 cities have public service internship programs, as do 25 county and 40 state agencies.

The New York City Urban Corps employs 7,000 political interns every summer. Almost half stay on in part-time jobs during the winter, attending college simultaneously. They work around the settlement houses, City Hall, borough halls, and state office buildings in Albany as well as in New York City.

Some New York interns have gone rapidly from campaign volunteer to research analyst to city government—from zero to as high as $18,000 per year, long before they have reached age 30.

And they feel so *good* about it!

"There isn't a book in the world that can teach you more about politics and the inner workings of government than a six month stint of actually working on the inside," John W. Holt, a former intern, now research analyst in New York City, told reporters Tom Poster and Alfred Miele of the *Sunday News*.

"You have more compassion for government after you've

been here," one California capitol intern told us. "You don't demand changes overnight."

Added another: "After a time working within government, you lose the feeling of being completely vulnerable."

"You go back to school and you hear the government is unresponsive—a common criticism," said a third person. "But when you're up here, you understand you must satisfy different people's demands, different people's interests."

The consensus of those who have taken part in government through an intern program is that one can't begin to appreciate the problems and solutions until one has been intimately involved.

How can you, a student, become involved in government through an intern program?

Begin by consulting your school counselor or your social science teacher. If no help is forthcoming from that sector, try your school or city library for information.

A selected list of internships and fellowships can be found in the back of this book, with application information included.

As an appendix to Frank Logue's study, the Ford Foundation lists summaries of seventy-four programs, in five sections: Executive Development Programs, Management Intern Programs, Experience-based Recruitment Programs, Academic-based Programs, and Programs Providing Exposure to Public Service. All of these sections offer internships and fellowships with goals of highly professional competency in commerce, economic development, business, labor, community affairs, urban development, politics, campaigning, and media—all government oriented.

The "granddaddy" of all the programs listed is the Coro Foundation, conceived in 1941 and operative since 1947. It is found within the section *Experience-based Recruitment Programs* and provides a structure through which Coro Fellows obtain a multiple perspective of public affairs. The interns work within all areas of public endeavor, rather than concentrating on one.

Coro Fellows and interns participate in a nine-month process called a *serial internship approach*, which simulates the pace and complexities of the public world. They spend four days a week in the field with people who are experienced in public affairs. They spend one day a week in seminar, sharing evaluations and planning field work.

Twelve fellowship positions per year are available in each of three Coro training centers: St. Louis, Los Angeles, and San Francisco.

Almost as old as the Coro Foundation is the program followed by the Department of Political Science, University of Kansas. Commencing in 1948 and funded by the state of Kansas under the heading Masters of Public Administration, the program is designed to develop dedicated and well-trained people to enter urban management.

Intern assignments include offices of administrative assistants to public managers, city managers, department heads, and agency staffs. Interns work on a two-year degree program, culminated by nine months in government.

The California Assembly Fellowship Program is the longest continuing state legislature intern program in the country. Coordinated since its beginning in 1957 by Vivian S. Miksak, admitted "den-mother" to the young interns, this program has trained 184 interns in the first 17 years of operation. Of these, 63 accepted staff positions with the Assembly for brief or extended periods following completion of the internship. Other post-internship activities have included public office, teaching, law, service with state and local governments, and graduate study.

Two current California assemblymen, Howard L. Berman of the 43rd (Beverly Hills and Hollywood Hills) District, and Barry Keene of the 2nd (North Coast, Redwood Empire,

Sonoma) District, were interns under Mrs. Miksak's program.

Berman was also an intern in the Office of Solicitor in the United States Department of Labor before he joined the California Assembly program. As an intern he was involved in legislative and research work on farm labor problems for the California Assembly Committee on Agriculture.

Barry Keene, following his internship, worked for five years as counsel to legislative committees and to the California Constitution Revision Commission.

Both Berman and Keene have become well known for their legislation in the environmental and health fields. Keene introduced a medical malpractice bill in 1975 which may have national importance; Berman is noted for his "no fault" insurance bill, among others.

The number of applicants for the California Assembly internships has risen steadily: 250 for the 1972-73 season; 404 for 1973-74. These internships are hard to come by: Out of 435 applicants for the 1975-76 year, only 10 were accepted, with 4 alternates. Of the 10, 6 were men, 4 women.

Accepted interns receive $764 per month for an eleven-month period. For this stipend they are expected to serve as full-time assistants to the Assembly, performing a variety of research and administrative assignments for committees and members in both Capitol and district offices.

Fellows reside in Sacramento from August through the following June, and are required to travel within the state on legislative assignments. Weekend and evening work may be (and usually is) required.

Along with their legislative duties, fellows are required to attend the seminars mentioned earlier. Group discussions and special readings and reports round out the interns' experience.

The success of the Assembly program has induced the California Senate to follow with their own prospectus, which has been drawn up with guidelines closely resembling the Assembly's.

The most important difference between the Senate and Assembly internships is the division by the Senate into six full-time and eleven part-time positions.

There is a contrast in Senate assignments from Assembly interns in that the full-time appointments serve only on standing committee staffs, while those accepted for part-time internships are assigned to individual senator's offices within the Capitol, none at district office level.

The full-time stipend is the same as the Assembly fellows, $764 per month; the part-time stipend is $135 per month, and the student is expected to attend classes at the University of California (Davis Campus) or California State University at Sacramento during the course of his or her internship.

Coordinator James R. McCauley is a special consultant to the Senate Rules Committee. He has worked out the details of the Senate program with Vivian Miksak's cooperation.

The Senate program has been three years in the formative stages, and over 350 full-time and 25 part-time applications were received by McCauley's office in its first year in operation.

Other internships are available within the Capitol in Sacramento. Some are strictly volunteer and unregistered, usually performed for college credit in an arrangement worked out between the individual lawmaker and a college professor. Still others pay only a token one-dollar-a-month fee, which is signed over by the intern to the Assembly Rules Committee; this registers the intern and puts him or her under state disability insurance in case of accident.

In response to our question about how many of these unregistered and dollar-a-month interns there might be, Vivian Miksak answered, "There is no telling. No way to find out. They come in droves in the summer. Some stay a week, some stay a month. But they all get some exposure to government in action."

Because of her long experience in the California Assembly Fellowship Program, Mrs. Miksak has often been called upon as consultant to new programs springing up nationwide.

As internship and fellowship programs began to expand in the late 1960s and early 1970s, a National Center for Public Service Internship Programs was established following a conference held in Lexington, Kentucky, in October, 1971. The center represents a broad spectrum of internship programs: local, state, regional, minority, university-affiliated, and national.

Under the leadership of Executive Director Richard Ungerer, a Directory of Internship Programs was presented for general distribution. The publication was prepared with the financial support of the National Urban Fellows.

According to a foreword in the 1975 Directory: "Plans are underway to improve information exchange by compiling the first complete data bank on internship funding, program design, and educational components."

The information gathered and computerized will be sent to members of the center through regular national newsletters and program catalogs.

Both federal and state lawmakers think highly of internships.

Assemblyman Bill Lancaster of California's 49th District has had interns working on his staff, and heartily endorses the program.

"Interns have been of great assistance to me," Lancaster declares. "In addition, I feel that the program has been of value to the intern, in that it gives him a better understanding of our legislative process. I would hope that the program would be expanded, as I feel it is of great value both to the legislator and the intern."

Alaska's Mike Gravel told us virtually the same thing.

"They are extremely helpful to the members, and the experience provides excellent on-the-job training for prospective staffers. I would like to see all such programs continued and expanded."

Gravel added, "I also think in-depth instruction in school on what members and staff do on a day-by-day, week-by-week basis would be helpful."

Searching for an answer to our question about staff training, Bella Abzug, New York City's well-known representative in Congress, confessed, "I know of no formal program."

She named the Democratic Study Group which has held weekend seminars for new staff members, ". . . and that was a good idea." The JFK Institute at Harvard she remembered as offering an introductory training period for new members of Congress. She recalled various manuals that provide technical advice on how the House operates.

"That's about it," she said.

"Except for the intern programs which are a godsend to members of Congress, and, also, I believe, very productive for the students."

Congress places some 50 intern/fellows every year through the American Political Science Association (APSA.) The main scope of recruitment is through national competition between political scientists, journalists, and other participants who apply through the APSA. A stipend of $7,500 is adjusted upward on the basis of the number of children dependent upon the participants.

The New York State Assembly Intern Program has expanded to carry 175 in three separate designs:

1. January Program —Intern term project. Full-time, four weeks.
2. Session Program —February-May. Part-time and full-time throughout Legislative Session.
3. Summer Program —Eight weeks, graduate students, intensive research; background must be appropriate to project.

Placements are Assembly-wide, including permanent staff offices which serve standing and fiscal committees. Stipends depend on program components, hours worked, academic level, and distance traveled. Session Components: $150-$350; Summer Program: $125 per week for eight weeks.

Younger students seeking internships may be "turned off" when they find most prerequisites include baccalaureate, Master's, and, in many cases, Doctorate degrees.

Have faith!

In 1970, Sharlene Pearlman Hirsch began *Executive High School Internships of America* in New York City, with twenty-five students and twenty-five corporate, governmental, or professional executive sponsors.

Dr. Hirsch told us that in 1975 a nationwide network of selected school districts from New York, New Jersey, Delaware, Colorado, Texas, Louisiana, Georgia, Tennessee, Kansas, Iowa, Illinois, Alabama, Massachusetts, Pennsylvania, Maryland, Florida, California, and Washington, D.C., enrolled participants in *Executive High School Internships.*

Of the more than 2,500 students in the 1975 program, one-half to one-third, depending on the locality, interned within the public sector as aides to judges, legislators, commissioners, sheriffs, mayors, council members, and county administrators.

Do high school students really work in these lofty positions?

"People are amazed," Sandra Verlinde, coordinator of the High School Interns Program in Sacramento, told us. "Accustomed to college interns, they see a high school student away from school all day, they ask, 'What are you doing here?' 'Why aren't you in school?' "

These individuals really work we discovered.

That was Sharlene Hirsch's original premise: Many students, bored by high school curricula, particularly graduating seniors with all subject requirements met, could invest their time more wisely by learning at firsthand the inner machinery of business, commerce, nonprofit agencies, mass communications, civic organizations, and, of course, government.

Students in the program, high school juniors and seniors, are released from all obligations to attend classes or make up work that has been missed *for the entire semester.*

We wondered if these were extraordinarily gifted students.

"No," Ms. Verlinde said. "The gifted student doesn't necessarily make the best intern. It is usually a person who has some self confidence, who says, 'Hey! I don't know what's out there, but I'd like to give it a try.' "

What else is needed? we pressed.

"He has to be able to talk to people. To be mature. To want to conform to a dress code without losing his own identity. He must have reading skills. Some may have a lot to learn in terms of discipline, but then, so do adults."

We spoke with some of the Sacramento interns who were working within the California state capitol complex.

"At first I was working for the Assembly Research Department," said Marian Gaston, a petite, vivacious, seventeen-year-old senior at John F. Kennedy High.

We thought she may have been put to filing in the research office.

"Oh, no," Marian protested. "I worked on research for Senator George Moscone, for a bill that would have all children going into first grade screened for disability impairment, and for the prevention of disability impairment."

How long did that assignment take?

"It took me about a month. I did a paper on that. I went to the health department, talked with senators and assemblymen, went to the library, interviewed people I knew who had made earlier reports on the subject."

Impressed, we turned to Ruth Rosenberg, also a senior

and seventeen, from McClatchy High. Ruth is dark-haired, quiet, thoughtful.

"Right now," Ruth said seriously, "I'm helping edit a book that I also helped research. It comes out of the governor's appointment section. It was mandated by the Maddy Registery Act, in which all members of boards and commissions appointed by the governor are listed. It is called the *Central Appointments Registry*. There is a fact sheet on each—about 240 of them—with all pertinent information noted. Then there is another section of appointments made by other elected officials, such as the attorney general, treasurer, controller, director of food and agriculture—two separate volumes."

"Would you like to continue in this line of work?" we asked.

"I plan to take political science at the University of California, Santa Cruz," Ruth answered. "Then I'd like to continue work in the governor's office. Or the office of planning and research. I'd like to go on there, if I could."

We turned back to Marian. "How about you?"

"Well, right now I'm working over in the Department of Employment Development," Marian replied. "I'm visiting the various sections, writing an outline of the functions of this very complex department. This will take me through my last day of the program. . . ."

"Would you come back to finish," we interrupted, "if you run out of time, just for the fun of having completed the job?"

"I probably would," Marian laughed, her dark eyes flashing. "It's been very enjoyable over there. I've enjoyed the experience so very much. I wouldn't exchange it for anything. I'd like to work there steadily."

Sandra Verlinde has witnessed great changes in her group within the few short months in which they were involved. Bored, often lethargic students became, almost overnight, self-motivated, eager, hard-working. Dormant leadership was awakened, and creativity abounded.

Sharlene Hirsch's Executive High School Internships Program has made its mark on Ms. Verlinde as well.

"Every day is a learning experience for me, too," she admitted as she talked of all the facets in business and government to which her students had been assigned. From interior designer to mortician; from working at the Chamber of Commerce to the School for the Deaf; from being at the sheriff's office to the State Capitol, Sandra Verlinde's charges have swiftly matured before her eyes.

"After fourteen years of teaching in the public schools, this is the most fascinating job that I could ever envision," she said.

Not all high school interns are suddenly smitten by an intense desire for a life in politics, we found.

We asked Brian Heilman, who had been working for Senator Albert Rodda, if his future had been changed in any way by his months in the California Capitol.

"I don't know yet what I want," Brian answered candidly. "I've considered the legal arena very carefully. I've considered politics, but not in the near future. I think we need men in the legislature with experience in all aspects of life, and not those who have just confined themselves to school and the political process without having reached out into other areas."

Brian, who will attend Columbia University, worked on waste control management while he was in Senator Rodda's office, researching the conversion of sewage and garbage into natural gas, creating a new industry in California.

Tim Titus, who plans a two-year mission for his church before entering Brigham Young University, became deeply involved with transportation for the handicapped. He correlated a photo-slide series on the issue, including many of his own photos.

"My report was to be presented to the Senate soon. Hopefully through my research something will be done for the handicapped. They've been without transportation until now."

Tim Titus also did a synopsis on legislative voting records and a study on dog-racing. He kept busy in his spare time by doing "a lot of constituent work."

Marian Gaston summed up the total experience of the young group of interns. "I'll tell you one thing—when I'm eighteen I'll take voting seriously. The experience of watching the Assembly in action. The Senate. You feel you know the person. He isn't just a name on the ballot. Or a person on television. He's real. I've learned so much. Things that have been around me all these years that I wasn't aware of. Now it's so obvious, it seems that everyone should know these things."

James R. McCauley, sitting in his office on the fifth floor of the Capitol Annex, offered some words of advice to the student who might be having difficulty in gaining an internship.

"The field is very competitive," he said. "Considering the number of students who apply, and the comparatively small number we accept, it goes without saying that a lot of well-qualified people will be turned away."

This shouldn't keep disappointed applicants from trying in other directions, McCauley insisted.

"They should volunteer," he said. "There are a lot of jobs to be done within the system. They should call on the caucuses—their party caucus, women's caucus, black, chicano—and offer their services as volunteers. This will get them into the places where they will meet the people in power, the people who will give them the paying jobs."

McCauley went on to list the places where volunteers are needed within the Capitol: reporting on the judicial; reporting on bills pending and bills in committee; watch-dog jobs; researching; communicating.

"We deal in communication here," he said. "The volunteer must have something to offer, must be able to read, to research, to write, to report, to communicate with the interested people."

McCauley stressed accuracy and objectiveness in research and reporting.

"If you're working for a member," he said, "researching for him, doing a study for him, you have to be able to give him a cool analysis. Be objective. Openminded. There is no room for personal prejudice. You've got to give the member the facts, the true facts without coloring them. Otherwise, you'll get your member in trouble, because he will be reporting or speaking about, or writing on the data you gave him."

When analyzed, James R. McCauley's words cover the whole spectrum of elective government. The entire political game should be based on *true fact*.

For you to do now:
Investigate the internships open to you now. Aim toward an internship open to you in the future. Follow the advice of James R. McCauley, above. If there is no official opening, make your own as a volunteer. Become active in any way possible. Activity is involvement. Don't be afraid to ask any elective official for a chance to become an intern or unpaid volunteer.

Chapter

11. WOMEN IN ELECTIVE GOVERNMENT

Wherever we went, whatever we read, to whomever we spoke during our research in this phase of our study, we were constantly aware of the new place for women in elective government.

Recent history shows us that women have always been on the political scene. On the scene, but barely tolerated; more often, they were rebuffed.

The last quarter of the twentieth century will see women not only coming into their own as a political force, but actually a spearhead for humanism, truth, honesty, and all that is "good" in self-government.

From the Daughters of Liberty, who were activists before the Revolution, to the proponents of the Equal Rights Amendment to the Constitution (ERA), the traditionally apolitical position of American women is slowly changing to one of power.

Or *Clout!* as Susan and Martin Tolchin named their book about woman power and politics.

Women have perenially been called upon to lend a little "softness" to hardbitten machine politics. After obtaining the right to vote, women were expected to bring out the PTA crowd and the Garden Club ladies, whose ballot—though minimal at first—soon became a potential force not to be ignored.

Women were endured in the New York, St. Louis, and Chicago political machines for the good they could do for the men in the higher echelons of their party.

An interesting study of the "Role and Status of Women in the Daley Organization," first appearing as a paper at the APSA annual meeting in Washington, D.C., September 1972, typifies the manner in which women were "allowed" to slowly work their way into the Chicago machine of Mayor Richard Daley.

So far, but no farther, according to Mary Cornelia Porter and Ann B. Matasar, authors of the paper.

Showing by scholarly research the general characteristics of "The Daley Woman"—she must first of all be loyal; if white, she may not be a WASP; if black, she need not be a Catholic; she must be involved with "womanly" community affairs—the authors conclude that the Daley organization is only interested in a woman's potential as a candidate if her sex fulfills a political function.

Caring about people, however, "does not preclude having a law practice, or a specialized knowledge of housing, or an interest in the rights of minorities—and women," wrote the authors. Their paper was reprinted in a collection of articles edited by Jane S. Jaquette, entitled *Women in Politics*.

Wondering "whether politics transcends sex, or merely ignores women," Jaquette writes in the preface to her book:

> Whether male dominance of what is conventionally seen as political activity is a result of our primate inheritance, natural dispositions, cultural norms, or enforced social sanctions, it is a fact. As a result, there has been little to say about women in politics and there are few women who have acquired prestige as political scientists or political theorists.

An additional fact is the way women as candidates are treated by the press and television. Always on the lookout for the "leggy" photographic view, the outlandish in dress, the unrestrained hysteria of "rights" gatherings, the media seems to treat women in any form of government as "freaks," rather than professionals.

In Washington, the media even treat their own as pariah; it wasn't until early 1975 that The Gridiron Club elected Helen Thomas of the United Press International as its first woman member. This move in effect slammed the door on such other talented journalists as Mary McGrory, Catherine Mackin, and Connie Chung, to name only a few who work the Washington beat.

Invitations to annual all-male newsmen's bashes or a dunk in a male-dominated pool might not seem high priority, but they are indicative, part of the pile of straws that has figuratively broken many a woman politician's back.

Women in ward politics, or city, state, or national politics, have been crying urgently for equal treatment. As the cries became strident—the *big screamers* is the way Republican women referred to demonstrators at the 1972 Democratic Convention—hostilities arose. Antipathy toward women in leadership of any social or political assemblages gave way to out-and-out animosity, and even spread to certain female factions.

Many leaders in the modern thrust toward women's rights have found themselves at odds with their sisters for tactical and ideological reasons.

Phyllis Schlafly, radio and television personality and an outspoken opponent of the Equal Rights Amendment, and Madeline Matchko, a labor lobbyist, who had successfully led a 1972 STOP-ERA defeat of ratification in the Connecticut legislature, are on one extreme end of a spectrum that includes Bella Abzug and Shirley Chisholm on the other.

Women can pull together, however. This was proved when a coalition between Judy Pickering's NOW (National Organization for Women, formerly headed by Betty

Friedan) and Michigan Representative in Congress Martha Griffith's ERA forces succeeded in winning the Connecticut ratification the following year. In 1975, though, pro-ERA forces were soundly defeated in New York and New Jersey.

Other coalescing among women's groups has been apparent in recent years, notably in Congress where such activists as Abzug, Chisholm, Yvonne Burke, Barbara Jordan, and Patsy Mink, to name a few, came together in a successful effort to include domestic workers among those eligible for minimum-wage protection.

Not all women in politics have been traditionally suffragists.

In 1920, during her first campaign for the office of representative in Oklahoma's 2nd District, Miss Alice Robertson, then sixty-six, told a curious gathering of male voters, "I have always done a man's work, carried a man's burden, and paid a man's bills. Whenever I needed help in money matters, I got a man to advise me."

She called the Nineteenth Amendment a "mess of pottage," and when elected to Congress, she voted against the Sheppard-Towner Bill (a maternity-infancy measure originally authored by Jeanette Rankin that called for, among other things, free hygiene instruction) and against the creation of the U.S. Department of Education. Miss Robertson ended her brief tenure in Congress after she angered the women's clubs and the Women's Auxiliary of the American Legion when she opposed a World War I veterans' bonus.

Another woman who would have been out of place among today's activists was Fannie Pearl Oldfield, who was nominated to fill her late husband's unexpired term in the 70th Congress. Having gained her seat through political strategy, she was never happy in her term of office. She yearned instead to be in "the sphere in which I believe women belong —the home."

"Widow Congressman" Frances Bolton, who was reelected fourteen times, was another story.

Wife of Representative Chester Bolton, the member from Cleveland, Ohio, lost her final election at the age of eighty-three, when redistricting cost her a loyal constituency.

Labeled "the richest woman in Congress," Frances Bolton used her wealth in exemplary ways. Her Washington staff was always the best paid and larger than the restrictions placed on it by House rules. She returned her pension check unsigned; she established nursing schools; she began the National Committee for the Study of Juvenile Reading; and she established research centers for the study of radio communication and parapsychology.

If her ideology for equal rights was apparent, it was primarily in the field of nursing. Before her husband's death, Frances Bolton was instrumental in establishing the Army School of Nursing; the $5 billion Bolton Act created the U.S. Cadet Nurse Corps.

As a representative, Frances Bolton fought for equality for Negro nurses, and in the sixties she sponsored an equal-rights-for-men bill, authorizing the commissioning of male nurses for the Navy and Army.

Congressman (a term she preferred) Bolton also favored the drafting of women, often saying, "Women's place includes defending the home."

With all of these divergencies in the past, it is no wonder that ideologists among women in the late 1970s seem to be too entangled for rational management.

Mrs. Abzug (a term *she* prefers) brought out the professional politician's viewpoint in *Bella*. Writing about her relationship with other women high up in the national women's rights picture, she says:

> Gloria Steinem, Shirley Chisholm and I have this major difference of opinion with Betty (Friedan, former head of NOW) as to what the nature of a women's political movement should be. She seems to think we should

support women for political office no matter what their views, and we don't. I feel our obligation is to build a real political movement of *women for social change.* [Abzug's emphasis.]

When she speaks of Betty Friedan's apparent pulling in the wrong direction from political success for the women's movement, Mrs. Abzug is quick to acknowledge Friedan's overall contribution to the cause, a "stimulation" that led to the formation of such groups as NOW. However,

. . . All I'm beginning to wonder is if she realizes that forming a political movement is a more complicated thing than giving lectures, writing books, having one-shot demonstrations and press conferences and appearing on the *Dick Cavett Show.*

The two-week (June, 1975) congress of more than 2,000 delegates in Mexico City for the International Women's Year experienced much the same frustration brought on by political differences and tactics found within the United States women's movement.

"The focus is too much on the uses to which women can be put, rather than women as individual human beings." Australia's Elizabeth Reid summed up the feelings of many at the United Nations-sponsored conference.

That there is a place in politics and elective government for women has been illustrated in many ways during the past few years.

With the naming of Carla Hills to fill the position of secretary of housing and urban development, important appointive posts reserved solely for men in the past opened up for women.

Alice Rivlin, former assistant secretary of health, education and welfare, was named director of the congressional office of the budget. This is perhaps the most important position Congress can appoint anyone to fill, according to Mrs. Rivlin's foremost backer, Senator Alan Cranston. Mrs. Rivlin, most recently a Senior Fellow at Brookings Institute, is a widely respected writer in the field of economics, budget alternatives, and social experimentation.

Women in other phases of government include Wallace Albertson, wife of Jack Albertson, the co-star of the television show *Chico and The Man*.

Mrs. Albertson was elected president of the California Democratic Council, and her husband's stardom had nothing to do with it. At the spring, 1975, convention of the CDC in Fresno, she proudly proclaimed, "I have paid my dues on the political scene." None could argue with her on that statement.

At twenty-seven Mrs. Albertson was assistant account executive in the Adlai E. Stevenson 1952 New York campaign for the presidency. In the twenty-three year existence of the CDC, Wallace Albertson, who moved to California in 1955, has been active for twenty years. Avowing a liberal philosophy, she helped found Women Strike for Peace, in Los Angeles. She headed Operation Bootstrap Interracial Dialogues following the 1965 Watts riots and chaired the Coalition for Fair Representation for Mexican-Americans.

"My personal commitment to social change is what drew me to the CDC in the first place," Wallace Albertson said in a postelection statement. "More importantly, I have acted upon controversial issues, where values and principles come into play."

Women at the grass roots level are getting ready for the next general elections. This was apparent during a political seminar held in Sacramento in February, 1975.

Organized by the local chapter of the National Women's Political Caucus, the seminar offered 8 workshops, each re-

peated three times to assure all 300 attending could partici-
pate. Topics covered were: Identifying the Issues and
Taking a Stand; Party Politics: How to Use Your Party;
Obstacles Within: The Politics of the Spirit; Gaining Com-
munity Support; Finances; Targeting the District; Political
Reform; National Politics; and The Media.

One of the biggest deterrents to women who would like
to break into politics is a lack of self-confidence, according
to the seminar consensus among women who already have
broken the mold. But the opportunity to educate the electorate and all with whom one comes in contact, not the least
of whom are other candidates, is a major factor in overcoming innate shyness.

"If you watch some men who have been elected to their
jobs," Betty Smith, vice-mayor of Chico (California), told a
luncheon crowd, "you soon realize that they ran for office
and were elected, and if *they* can do it, so can you."

And if you lose an election, Helen Putnam, mayor of
Petaluma, commented, it doesn't mean everyone in the community is against you. "It just means that yours is a minority
point of view. Just don't ever let it dawn on you that you
can't do it."

Many women never let the possibility of defeat deter
them from their goals.

The 94th Congress convened with seventeen women—
fourteen Democrats and three Republicans—all in the House
of Representatives.

Conversely, three women senatorial candidates went down
(temporarily): Democrats Barbara Mikulski, Maryland;
Betty Roberts, Oregon; and Republican Gwenyford Bush,
South Carolina.

But there were winners in other areas of government.

Ella Grasso, a veteran campaigner from Connecticut,
took top honors when she was named Democratic governor.

New York State Senator Mary Anne Krupsak won the

position of lieutenant governor against the wishes of the Democratic hierarchy, teaming with victorious Hugh Carey in his sweep to the governor's chair.

Susie Sharp of North Carolina became the first woman chief justice of a state supreme court; Janie Shores became the first woman supreme court justice in Alabama.

Legislators elected at state level included a Roman Catholic nun, Clare Dunn of Tucson, Arizona; and Geraldine Travis, the first black woman in Montana's legislature.

Republican Millicent Fenwick, who later was to make history when she toured Indochina with an eight-member congressional delegation, went counter to a trend in New Jersey when she defeated Democrat Fred Bohen.

Kansas Democratic Representative Martha Keys, a leader in the 1972 McGovern campaign, went to Congress with her brother-in-law, Gary Hart, the new Colorado senator, also a big man in the McGovern entourage.

These are only a few of the names you will read about in future political stories. Along with Marjorie Holt, Elizabeth Holtzman, and Margaret Heckler, these women will become as well known as Abzug, Chisholm, Jordan, Margaret Sanger, and Susan B. Anthony.

How does a "Political Woman" differ from a political man, or from her apolitical sisterhood?

A book carrying the above title, written by Georgetown University political science professor Jeanne J. Kirkpatrick, surveys forty-six women, all of whom had been elected at least twice to the legislature of their respective states.

Dr. Kirkpatrick discovered that the women politicians she studied—they averaged forty-eight years of age and were mothers twice on average—were less likely to see their elective office as a stepping stone to either higher office or financial betterment. She found them more committed to a moralist conception of politics than their male colleagues, and more willing to work toward the public good, which characteristic made them less subject to flattery, more virtuous, and less inclined to be swayed by lobbies or pressure groups.

In most cases, the woman legislator ran for office as an extension of many years of volunteer community service, ". . . because a lifetime of concerned citizen activism convinced her that political office is the only viable means of implementing the programs and changes she wants to see in her community."

Women of character are widely sought in the filling of commission posts. One extraordinary black woman has been named chairman of the New York City Commission on Human Rights by two mayors, John Lindsay in 1970 and Abraham Beame in 1974.

Eleanor Holmes Norton spent her childhood in Washington, D.C., gaining insight on social justice and discrimination. A history major at Antioch College, she received her J.D. from Yale, picking up a history master's on her way.

In accepting her appointment, Mrs. Norton put forth the strong ethic that has made her so respected in her position.

"As commissioner," she said, "I will attempt to see that no man is judged by the irrational criteria of race, religion, or national origin."

Her record has shown that she wasn't simply voicing platitudes. Among her strong stands for human rights, Eleanor Norton's 1968 defense of George Wallace's right to use New York's Shea Stadium for a political rally is unimpeachable evidence of her integrity.

In an interview with Barbara Kashian Gubbins for *Tuesday at Home* (November 30, 1974), Mrs. Norton saw today's young women breaking preconceived barriers—if they don't "play themselves short." They should "prepare themselves to be what they genuinely believe they can be," she said.

"They [the barriers] have got to be broken at some time, and these young people may be the first young people in America to have the opportunity."

March Fong Eu was born in a room behind a Chinese laundry in Oakland, California.

In 1974 she was elected by one of the largest votes in California history to the office of secretary of state, after several successful years in the Assembly.

We asked Mrs. Eu for words of advice to the upcoming generation of women who may be inclined toward the world of elective government.

"I think there are just great opportunities for women today. I think the Equal Rights Amendment, the women's movements, have all opened a great many doors to all people in our society, and women included, because women have been second class citizens for so long now. So I'm urging women to get involved. They don't all have to run for public office, of course. They can get involved in their own way. But at least they can feel that they are no longer second class citizens, and they have a right to do what they want to do."

"Have you noticed a change in the number of young women taking staff positions within elective government?" we asked.

"I think things are changing dramatically, and I think a lot of men are looking for women to work in their offices," March Eu answered. "I think that their eyes are suddenly opened, that they've got a large segment of society that they've neglected for a long time. I think the opportunities are just overwhelming."

Young women are preparing themselves, and are taking advantage of this new opportunity to play an active part in self-government.

We saw them in the conventions; we spoke with them in

the convention halls and in the corridors of the capitols. They are eager. They are inspired. They are committed. These impressions will never leave us.

Young women are sure that they stand on the threshold of a new, vibrant America. They are not afraid of the old taboos, of too-powerful machine bosses, of older women who have exhausted themselves in waging the good fight.

We met women in politics in many roles. Some were volunteers. Some were underpaid. Some had reached professional levels where personal fiscal responsibilities could be met realistically.

They all shared one trait: optimism!

Politically committed women have a great deal of optimism about their own personal future, the future of their families, and most important, the future of America.

For you to do now:
If you are a young woman, seek out your nearest women's political organization.
If you are a young man, do what is within your power to reinforce the young women within your own personal sphere as they become involved in elective government.

Chapter
12. A CONCISE SKETCH OF THE PARTY SYSTEM

"The political party is the only basic form of democratic process we have. . . ."

These are not the words of a nationally known political figure. They voice the sincere thoughts of Dwayne Adams, president of the California Young Democrats, as he spoke with us during the tumult of the 1975 Democratic Central Committee convention in Sacramento's new Community Center.

Adams' quotation sums up our study of political parties: their place within our system of government, the necessity for a strong adversary movement to subsist between two major parties, and the place for young people within the system.

In our social studies and civics classes we learned all about the forming of the party system in the United States: how the minor parties surfaced and disappeared, and how the two major parties that today form the base in our elective process evolved.

The major parties of the earliest days of our republic were the Federalists and the Anti-Federalists, the Whigs and the Democratic Republicans, and the National Republicans and the Jacksonian Democrats.

The Anti-Masonics and the Abolitionist Liberty Party, the Free-Soil Party, the American (Know-Nothing) Party, and

Horace Greeley's Liberal Republicans, all had their brief moments in nineteenth-century American history.

Conditions remain unchanged today.

The 1972 national election saw the following "third" parties running candidates for the presidency: American First, American Independent, Communist, Libertarian, People's Party, Prohibition, Socialist Labor, Socialist Workers, and Universal.

Of these parties, the Prohibition Party is the oldest, having entered elections since 1869.

Other old-timers include the People's Party, also known as the Populists, which began campaigning in 1892. The Socialist Labor Party began in 1877, but didn't enter its first national contest until 1892. The Workers Party was formed after a series of splits among the Socialists, and began campaigning in 1921; later it was to become the Communist Party after another ideological schism.

The elections of 1978 or 2000 will offer no diminution in numbers of minor parties.

Third parties take as much time and commitment as major parties. Perhaps more dedication is required, because historically third parties are notoriously underfinanced and understaffed. However, within the makeup of our national political scene, third parties offer many tangible assets.

In *We Elect a President*, David E. Weingast wrote:

> Some ideas that began in the platform of third parties have later been adopted by Democratic and Republican leaders. Third parties have again and again complained that major parties have pirated their principles. Many of the humanitarian and social policies that today are accepted practice in the United States were once the property of third parties. These include:
> the eight-hour day
> protection for women and children in industry
> workmen's compensation
> unemployment insurance

old-age pensions
government-supported education
government-supported housing
tenement-house and factory inspection
a federal program for medical care

Each party, large or small, has its own ideology. Each has its program and candidates to sell. And each has its dedicated and involved membership.

Each also has its media-oriented consultants, who for a fee will present the message in the most forceful and, at the same time, most seductive, alluring, and palliating manner.

For our purposes, a concise sketch of the party system must include these "workers behind the scenes," as well as the "pols" seeking voter recognition. For it is within these planning and staging areas that many job opportunities await the young person eager to plunge headlong into elective government.

The pulsating heart of the party system is found in the convention hall, and in the adjoining "rooms" where members caucus within easy access to party hierarchy.

These rooms—usually smaller meeting areas within the main hall complex—were formerly called "smoke-filled" because of the closed-door policy that marked their rise to prominence in party policymaking. More recently these rooms have been thrown open to the fresh air of public scrutiny as members of all parties have moved—on face value—toward the expediency of high moral obligation to the electorate.

The political party convention brings together people of mutual purpose. They come together to consolidate their philosophy through debate and decide upon individuals to carry their standards before the general populace at election time.

The excitement engendered in a convention is unlike that

to be experienced anywhere. Except for a national presidential nominating convention (and there are those who say it surpasses that), the most exhilarating gathering is an off-year state central meeting. Jockeying for position here within the state organization can often lead to national recognition in the political future.

The most important state conventions are held in the most populous states—Illinois, Ohio, Pennsylvania, New York, California. These are the states where swing votes— and heavy donations—could normally be expected. Despite recent legislation to discourage "big money" from swelling campaign funds, these large states have not lost their importance on the political landscape.

When the California Democrat and Republican Central Committees both selected Sacramento for their biennial get-together, the occasion to witness two of the most viable and influential political organizations in action within a two-week span brought interested observers from all over the country.

The programs listed as speakers senators, representatives, governors, and state constitutional officers by the dozens. In what is a supposedly off-year in national politics, no fewer than five Democratic hopefuls for the presidency pressed their qualifications on the curious ears of the 1,000 delegates and more than 1,000 observers.

The nation's press was well represented and the three major television networks were kept busy day and night, taping interviews and filming major speakers.

A candidate for the Republican ticket, ex-Governor Ronald Reagan, told an enthusiastic luncheon crowd—amid waving placards and shouts of "We Want Reagan"—why it was important to discourage third-party talk and instead build up strength in the party to which they were all philosophically bound.

A similarly enthusiastic luncheon crowd, two weeks earlier, was pleased when Edmund G. (Jerry) Brown, Reagan's successor, spoke only a few words without notes, and then threw the program open to questions from the floor.

Following that luncheon, we strolled along with a score of happy Democrats keeping step with the young governor as he made an amiable circuit of the center's curving walkways on his way back to his capitol office across the street.

These are just a few of our memories of two conventions.

While we weren't so much interested in party ideology, per se, and attempted to remain objective throughout both conventions, there was never any doubt in our mind that Republicans and Democrats are equally motivated by deeply held convictions.

What seems more important to us now, however, are the talks we had with young people involved with the conventions' operations, and our often too brief conversations with people working within the framework of the process.

Terri Jones, for example.

Terri was coordinator for the Democratic Convention. All problems, large or small, usually end up on the shoulders of the person holding that title.

We first saw Terri Jones on a Friday night, at an "open house" hosted by announced presidential candidate Lloyd Bentsen, senator from Texas, in one of the upper suites of the vast new Sacramento complex.

Terri, a slightly built woman in her twenties, scurried around, arms loaded with notes, harassed. There was good California white wine on the serving tables, and Jack cheese with tasty crackers, largesse for Democrats who came to meet the Texas senator. Terri was passing up all the goodies, a questing look shadowing her eyes, her blond hair undone, her long gown soiled from being stepped on.

We saw her again at eleven the next morning, on the stage of the main convention hall, arms still loaded with papers, eyes still haunted.

We stopped her for a moment, and heard how she had worked for Congressman John Burton, outgoing chairman of the Central Committee, and with the firm of Jeanmarie Maher and Associates, political consultants with offices in San Francisco.

Her title as coordinator is "administrative assistant" and she told us, brushing back her hair with a forearm, "I guess you have to be a little stupid to take this job."

We told Terri that we had observed her working hard the day before, to which she replied, "I worked from eight yesterday morning until midnight, then I was up early to come down here to the hall, and I'll probably be here until midnight tonight."

We asked her what she would be doing when the convention was over, and the party offices had changed hands.

She looked at us as though it was a question that required no answer.

"I'm going to be scrambling around, in search of a new job. Oh, yes. It will be within the political arena. It gets in your blood. Long hours. Poor pay. Abuse! Hah. . . ."

And Terri Jones was off, down into the crowd of brightly dressed, politicking Democrats that milled around the huge hall.

In the morning Dwayne Adams is a student at California State University, Sacramento, majoring in public administration. In the afternoon he works as a part-time legislative aide on the Assembly Committee on Juvenile Justice.

"I handle bills that have to do with youths and juveniles, amendments to the penal code, or introduce new legislation," Adams told us. "I'm also involved with the college Young Democrats, because I believe every young person when he's in college should learn about government. And the only way he can actually learn is by participating in a political party."

Adams, who plans to study law and eventually go into

elective government as a candidate, has been in party politics since he attended his first national convention at the age of sixteen.

He has been learning along with other people his age that "the party" is the best way to go.

"I think we learned a lesson during the 1967 Hippie Revolution that you can't freeload. It takes money. Then in the 1972 national convention we learned that you can't just come in and kick out old party regulars, because you're going to lose their vote. We're going to have to play the game. We're going to have to work within the system."

Two weeks later, we spoke with Paul Cheverton, seventeen-year-old president of the Claremont Junior Republicans and vice-president of the California Student Republican organization. Paul's major concern was starting clubs at high schools throughout the state.

"There is a great volunteer work-potential in student clubs," Paul Cheverton told us at the information table he had set up just outside the main convention hall. "People are slowly becoming aware of politics at the high school level. If we can bring them into the Republican Party now, there is a better chance of keeping them. And there is a great need to bring youth into the Republican Party, as witness the last election, 1972."

Alluding to the countless number of volunteer man-hours that can be realized from student organizations, Paul pointed out his own contribution.

"I wasn't able to vote legally because of my age. Yet in the last election through my volunteer work—driving, telephone work, house-to-house—I was probably able to vote a hundred times."

Paul, who wants to make politics a career, but secondary to a career in medicine, has definite ideas about the worth of schools and school organizations in educating young people about government.

"There has to be an opportunity for students to become involved. Good government teaching, American history—making sure that students really know how government functions."

Paul Cheverton was thoughtful for a moment.

"And somehow," he added, "there must be more importance put on how much their own vote counts. Many people think 'One vote? What's one vote? It's not going to change the world.' And when their man loses, they become apathetic. I think it's important that people want to work for a cause they believe in. As far as I can see, the best way is through the local party organization."

We approached Republican Congressman Barry Goldwater, Jr., before a committee meeting in one of the Community Center caucus rooms, and asked for his ideas on how young people can be turned on to elective government.

"I think," he answered, "the responsibility lies in the hands of the politicians and elected officials, that we begin being honest in our approach and explanations to the problems of the country. That we start telling them what the truth is, instead of telling them what they want to hear, and selling them a bunch of snake oil. Tell them the things that they've got to be told. Things, perhaps, that they don't want to hear about the situation in this country. Honesty, integrity, is going to help our political posture in the minds of the youth, more than anything I know of."

Two weeks before, we had asked the same question of Democratic Senator Alan Cranston. His answer, given in the comparative quiet of a near-empty Community Center press section, follows:

I believe very strongly that young people should get into government in Washington, D.C., and at other levels elsewhere. I worked in the government at a very tender age—I was in my twenties—I worked around Capitol Hill, on Capitol Hill, in the Executive Branch, during World War II. And that gave me the knowledge and insight and inspiration and concern that ultimately led me to the United States Senate. A lot of young people can follow that same path, and can play a part in the decision-making process.

There is no better system than Democracy. Ours is imperfect; we've got to make it work better. If we don't pay attention to it, if young people don't pitch in with their commitment and concern, we could go down the path to totalitarianism.

And that would be terrible for all the people in our country, young and old.

When young people do become involved in party politics, they can either run for office themselves or they can work for candidates through their party.

The latter is the route taken by several people with whom we spoke during the course of the two California conventions.

Joe Cerrell, who heads a Los Angeles-based political consulting firm, was personally leading a contingent working for Texas' Senator Lloyd Bentsen, one of the first Democrats to put forth a 1976 challenge to the Republican presidential incumbency.

"Joe has been active in party politics since 1954," an aide informed us before we were introduced. At that time, according to the aide, he helped Jesse Unruh, current California state treasurer and former Assembly speaker, in a local election try. Joe was a student at the University of Southern California at the time; since then he has become a nationally known force in political circles.

"Joe was executive secretary to Jerry Brown's father, Pat, when he was governor," the aide continued. "He was very close to Lyndon Johnson. He ran Hubert Humphrey's 1972 Pennsylvania and California campaigns. A lot of assemblymen here in Sacramento owe their jobs to Joe Cerrell," the aide confided.

Joe Cerrell, professionally affable, genuinely interested in our project, told us how much he had used young people within his organization.

"It sounds corny to say it," Joe smiled, shouting somewhat to be heard above the din of the big auditorium, "but I've had interns working with me since 1959. I've always been big on them. We bragged in the primary how low the average age was in our operation. Under thirty. About half and half, men and women."

Following a few more friendly affirmations concerning the need for young people in politics and in Joe Cerrell's Democratic Party business affiliations, we set out with Dick Rosengarten, the convention's press liaison man, to meet with some of them.

Dick worked for Cerrell "on and off" since 1970, after several years of newspaper writing in Los Angeles. After the June primary of 1974, he became "what I guess you'd call a political public relations type," and started his own business.

A hard-working young man in his late twenties, Dick Rosengarten typifies the tireless press person who knows everyone by name, answers all requests with immediate action, and keeps his good humor intact throughout a hectic weekend of party conventioneering.

Mardi Gregory, to whom Dick Rosengarten introduced us, holds a master's degree in communication from the University of California at Los Angeles. She is a part of Joe Cerrell's staff working on the Senator Bentsen assignment.

"I admire and respect the senator tremendously," she told us. "We first met him last spring when he came out to California as the chairman of the Senate Democratic Campaign Committee. We were fortunate enough to be involved with some of his tours. We met him and liked him and he liked us. And I think we work very effectively together."

Mardi is a dark-haired, enthusiastic young woman, with lively dark eyes which flash under the bright lights of the convention hall. Among her other duties, she writes speeches, statements, and releases, and does all-around media work.

We wondered if Mardi Gregory was happy in her career choice.

"This is very exciting," she cried out over the noise of the loudspeaker that was raucously calling the hall to order. "I really enjoy it very much."

We asked Harvey Englander to step outside the main hall, away from the hubbub of the politicking going on inside.

Harvey had introduced Mardi Gregory to Joe Cerrell, and had suggested that she apply when a job opening came up. Party ties bind through all levels, we were discovering.

Englander—not yet twenty-five at the time of our meeting—was working the convention for Joe Cerrell as a freelance public relations person.

"I worked for Joe for some six years," he related, "starting when I was eighteen, in the Hubert Humphrey campaign, as an office boy in Cerrell Associates, Inc. I left last July when I was twenty-four. I was corporate vice-president. I decided to go free-lance."

Harvey is of medium height, well-built, self-assured, and dedicated to the Democratic Party and to anyone for whom he works.

"You've got to work for people you believe in," he said. "Otherwise, you can't win."

We started to talk about party activity, finding a cause and a philosophy, and we branched off into the subject of campaigning.

Here, we were to discover, was another facet in elective government in which careers could be built.

For you to do now:
Locate any party headquarters in your vicinity. Ask them to explain what their party stands for. If their philosophy matches yours, offer your services as a volunteer.

Chapter
13. CAMPAIGNING

Hopes. Dreams. Triumphs. Defeats. Excitement. Joy. Sadness. Depression. Fun.

All of these sensations and impressions—and many, many more—are felt by anyone who, even in the most remote way, involves himself or herself with elective campaigning.

According to our study, campaigning is absolutely the quickest, easiest, and best way for a beginner to break into politics and elective government. And the doorway is clearly labeled: Volunteer!

Most of the people we spoke with, people considered professionals in campaign management, started as volunteers.

All officeholders—from nonpaid school board members to senators and representatives—had done some volunteer campaigning in their past. Legislative assistants, administrative aides, executive secretaries, and political workers of all types and responsibilities have campaigning listed in their resumes.

Harvey Englander, collaborating with Joe Cerrell on Senator Lloyd Bentsen's presidential campaign, started his career as a volunteer.

"I was in junior college in Los Angeles," he told us. "It was 1968, early spring. I was seventeen at the time. I had a professor in Political Science 101—his term paper assignment was to go and get involved in a political campaign and write about it. So I went to work for Bobby Kennedy."

Englander's term paper led to his first job with Cerrell Associates when he was eighteen. Since then he has worked exclusively in campaigns. He has never worked on any legislative staff.

"I've been in national presidential campaigns," he related. "I've traveled this country running campaigns." He talked fast, as is his nature. "Pennsylvania, Florida, Wisconsin, Oregon, California. Hubert Humphrey campaigns in 1968 and '72. Bobby Kennedy in 1968."

Harvey Englander's eyes flashed as he relived experiences.

"One of my main activities in politics is schedule and advance. . . ."

Schedule and advance, it seems, is handled by the person who goes to a locality ahead of the candidate and turns out large crowds in the most desirable environment, mainly through individual efforts and communication know-how.

". . . I've been introduced as Hubert Humphrey's favorite schedule and advance man. . . ."

Englander is off to other campaigns.

". . . In Oregon I ran a special election that everyone said we would lose. It was the Tuesday before Christmas. A morality-obscenity issue. We won by 40 votes out of 3,300 cast. Everyone said we were going to lose it by 2,000 votes."

He smiled broadly and repeated, "We won it by forty. That, I must say, was one of my highlights. In the little city of Medford, Oregon."

Listening to Harvey Englander, we were convinced that a campaigner can become just as excited over a vote on issues, even in retrospect, as a vote for office.

Campaigning is becoming big business, and not only big, but *sophisticated* big business. This is evidenced by the proliferation of campaign workshops being conducted around the country.

One of the most complete of these workshops was scheduled for July 10-12, 1975, at Kent State University, Kent, Ohio.

Named the "Political Campaign Management Institute," it was sponsored by the Department of Political Science and the Division of Continuing Education at the university. The institute staff included such nationally known campaign leaders as John D. Deardourff, Robert A. Strong, and Tony May.

Among his clients Deardourff counts governors James A. Rhodes, William Milliken, and Christopher S. Bond; senators Charles McC. Mathias, Richard S. Schweiker, Edward Brooke, Charles H. Percy, and Robert Stafford; and representative Pierre S. du Pont.

Tony May, president of May and Associates, Inc., is Director of Communications, Kent State, and is well known in campaign circles for his work with the 1972 Edmund S. Muskie presidential campaign.

Bob Strong is a vice-president of Campaign Associates, Inc., a Topeka, Kansas, organization that also conducts workshops and publishes a semimonthly overview of political techniques, *Campaign Insight*, the first of its kind.

Professional campaign managers and their staff personnel pay from $160 to $195 per person to attend programs such as those offered by the Kent State Institute and Campaign Associates. In three days of concentrated study, the participants learn the latest techniques in influencing the voter and selling the candidate.

Subjects in the Kent State program included the initial planning function, voting trend analysis and targeting, professional public opinion survey research, issue research, scheduling and advance, information gathering and data analysis, advertising, graphics, fund raising, the function of campaign headquarters, grass roots activities, and volunteers and recruitment. There is something for everyone in the study of campaigns and campaign management. And there is usually enough work to keep the professional campaign worker busy.

We asked several pros about job security, because it seemed to us that big national campaigns—the ones that had the large bankrolls—were spaced too far apart, and the pickings in local elections not lucrative enough to offer a dependable income for the worker.

"There's always an election of some kind," Mardi Gregory stated. "Seats to be filled in special elections; a legislator dies and his seat must be filled. Bond elections, school board elections. There always seems to be something going on in politics."

We heard the same thing from Ann Blumlein, a bright and personable woman in her midtwenties, who is with the San Francisco consulting firm known as The Bradley Group.

Ann never intended to become involved with professional campaign work. While an undergraduate in political science at Stanford University, she had gained firsthand exposure to practical politics as an intern in the Stanford-in-Washington program. After college, Ann told us, "I was fortunate enough to be accepted into the Coro intern program."

She did the Coro series of internships—politics, labor, government, business, media, and community organization— which, Ann said, is "Coro's way of looking at a municipality and the major elements which govern the municipality."

While she admitted that she wasn't able to study these subjects in depth, she said, "I knew a little more about each than when I started, and much more about how all these elements interact with each other when it comes to governing a city or even a small rural area."

When Ann Blumlein was in Coro, she did her political assignment with the McGovern campaign in San Francisco.

"I had some very good tutelage under the Democratic county chairman, made some good friends, some good contacts. I pursued my friendships, and found myself getting more and more interested in politics, acknowledging that politics pretty well pervades government no matter where you go."

After spending some time with the Democratic Central Committee in the spring, Ann attended the 1973 summer portion of Coro at Occidental College, where she prepared her master's thesis in urban studies.

"When I came out of that," she said, "I was looking for some kind of spot on a legislative staff. Something in the role of administrative assistant. However, in the fall of 1973 most of the incumbents and aspirants were looking for campaign staff, not legislative staff."

So Ann joined in the "Senator Bob Moretti for Governor of California" campaign, following a "trial run" in a state proposition.

"Proposition 1 was Governor Reagan's initiative," she remembered. "Moretti was the leader in fighting that. We were successful in defeating the initiative, and went into the governor race."

She smiled ruefully. "We were not quite that successful." It was the primary campaign that saw California's Governor Edmund G. Brown, Jr., emerge as a political power.

Ann Blumlein found her own personal success-quotient had risen in the ill-fated Moretti race, however, when she was asked to participate in another statewide campaign: that of William Norris for attorney general.

"I worked in the Northern California office," she recalled, "doing press work, advance and scheduling, staff coordination, volunteer coordination, fund raising. Absolutely a broad base."

Again her man lost. But Ann's work drew the attention of Don Bradley.

"For the first time I will be working for an established political consulting firm," Ann Blumlein happily told us, "as a part of Mr. Bradley's staff running the campaign of Senator George Moscone for mayor of San Francisco."

We inquired as to what her duties would include.

"I don't know what I'll be doing—probably a little bit of everything."

Ann Blumlein laughed. We had the feeling it didn't really matter what she would be doing. She had found her niche.

George Moscone won his election; thanks in no small part to Ann Blumlein and The Bradley Group, he is mayor of San Francisco.

The use of professional consultants and advertising agencies has played a major part in local, state, and national campaigns in recent years.

Pioneered by the firm Campaigns, Inc. (Clem Whitaker, reporter, lobbyist, and public relations man, and Leone Baxter, Chamber of Commerce manager, in 1933 established this long-lasting husband-wife partnership), such names as Spencer-Roberts, Lennen and Newell, Gaynor and Ducas, and J. Walter Thompson became synonymous with political consultation over the decades that followed.

The cost of image-making, of television and newspaper space, and of "special events" in campaigning has risen in direct proportion with the use of the professional consultants. Although the billion dollar bottom-line on campaign costs has caused no small amount of concern among candidates and voters alike, there is little chance of the total diminishing.

The Campaign Finance Act, signed into law by the president on October 15, 1974, will unquestionably be felt within the profession as a restraint, if not total reform.

Individual spending limitations for presidential, Senate and House general elections; contribution limits for parties and individuals; strengthened ties on corporate gifts; and the introduction of public financing all combine to make it more difficult for campaign funding to be funneled into well-laundered accounts that often were more corrupting than benevolent.

It is undeniable, however, that professionalism—honorable professionalism—is practiced within the ranks of election consultants.

The use of "telephone banks" or "boiler rooms"—where volunteers call voters at random or by plan—should not be considered as unprofessional.

Walking house-to-house, by either a candidate or a volunteer, should not be considered demeaning.

Boldly asking the constituent for his or her vote should not be embarrassing to either candidate or campaign worker —or to the voter either, for that matter.

Yet many a citizen who feels he or she holds the answer to the problems of the neighborhood, the city, the state, or the nation holds back his or her candidacy through reticence or downright bashfulness.

The only way to win an election is to ask for the vote!

The only way to represent your thinking, and the thinking of your friends and neighbors, is to win an election.

Whether you are seeking the office of the presidency of the United States or the office of school board trustee, the game is played the same.

We asked Tom Du Hain, at twenty-two the youngest member ever elected to a California Community College Board, what young people should do to affect local government.

"Don't be shy," was Tom's advice. "Go to meetings. Let yourself be heard. Be willing to spend time in government."

Tom Du Hain's campaign for one of the state's 600 college board seats came from his own conviction that he had something to offer.

A radio and television weathercaster with the famed Harry Geise Company, Tom received his Third Class broadcaster's ticket when he was a sixteen-year-old high school debater. Tom met Geise (who has become internationally known for his so-called "impossible" long-range weather forecasts) when he went to work for KCRA-TV, Sacramento, while still a college student.

Several years later, Du Hain's friends persuaded him to consider a nonpartisan, nonpaying opening on the Los Rios District Board (30,000 student enrollment, $3 million budget).

"The idea appealed to me," Tom told us, "because of my feelings about keeping community colleges tuition free, and because I think that someone from the broadcast media could bring expertise for informing the community about the benefits of their local college."

Tom Du Hain's was not a big money, professionally handled campaign. Heidi Ehrmann, a college friend, acted as manager. Roger Smith, who had a little experience in local politics, agreed to do publicity. A twenty-two-year-old candidate with a twenty-two-year-old manager and a twenty-seven-year-old publicist.

Du Hain went into hock $2,000, which guaranteed the operational budget.

"We took press releases and photos to all 30 newspapers within the five-county district," Tom recalled. "We printed 13,000 postcards to be sent out by individuals to their friends, neighbors, and relatives, asking for the vote. We made 5,000 copies of an article published in the Sacramento University *Hornet* that was very fair to our philosophy. We duplicated our press clippings and stapled all the material together to make a single handout."

Hitting the shopping centers, signing autographs, and calling on volunteer assistants from the two most populous counties, Sacramento and El Dorado, the Du Hain team blitzed the election, winning handily, tallying almost 30,000 votes against the runner-up's 10,500.

"I still haven't met all the volunteers," Tom confessed to us months after the campaign. "And strangely, considering my age, our most enthusiastic support came from people between forty-five and sixty."

One grey-haired grandmother-type, Du Hain recalls, demanded 500 packets of material to pass out among fellow club members and in her own neighborhood.

There is a punchline to follow this story. Not only did Tom Du Hain advance the money from his savings to get his campaign underway, but he had to take an enforced two-month air silence from his broadcasting job to comply with the equal-time campaign laws. His familiar voice and smiling face could not be heard or seen without allowing his opponents equal time, whether he was talking about the weather, the news, or his school board aspirations.

Guidelines set in the Fairness Doctrine and Section 315 of the Federal Communications Act, plus the Campaign Expenditures Limitation Law which became effective April 7, 1972, have done much to equalize the chances of understaffed, undercapitalized candidates.

Hank Parkinson, in his book *Winning Political Campaigns With Publicity,* goes one step farther as he shows the uninitiated "Clyde Candidate" how to exploit the media.

Parkinson, president of Campaign Associates and publisher of *Campaign Insight,* feels that in gaining publicity the most important communications tool is used.

In his book, Parkinson points out the many ways news space can be grabbed in the daily and weekly papers; how radio can be milked; and how to take advantage of television exposure.

If you are lucky enough to be asked to stand before the television cameras, according to Parkinson, it is wise to be prepared with a few dry runs with a tape recorder, particularly listening to the way you pronounce words.

"To do a good job," he writes, "you've only got to keep

three things in mind: be rested and relaxed, be cool and confident, and be prepared and concise."

Ever since television became the number one exposure medium, candidates and office-holders from the president down have had to become "actors" in front of the most critical audience in the world—the American voter.

One White House aide has as his sole responsibility the proper stage-managing of the president, for which he receives an annual salary of $36,500. (This precedent was set by President Eisenhower in 1952, when he selected suave filmstar Robert Montgomery as his television coach.) The judgment of whether or not the aide succeeds in this job is left to the pitiless scrutiny of millions of viewers every time a press conference is held or a president "talks" from the Oval Office.

Often it is better *not* to be seen on the merciless tube.

During Tom Du Hain's campaign, one opponent heard Tom's name mentioned in an offhand manner during KCRA's informal "Noon Show," along with the fact that Tom was running for election.

The opponent insisted on equal time.

Several days later, "Noon Show," on which Du Hain would normally appear were it not for his "air silence," graciously gave the opponent several minutes to state his qualifications, free of charge.

In contrast to Du Hain's professionalism, well-remembered by the viewers, the opponent appeared ill-at-ease, mumbled his lines, stumbled in reading his prepared speech, and was written off as a potential trustee of the Los Rios College Board.

In some markets where viewers are flooded with political aspirants—Chicago, New York, Philadelphia, Los Angeles— and VHF and UHF channels are packed with campaign messages, the television medium is best ignored and other approaches followed.

Bill Bond proved this when he ran for the Assembly from the 39th (Long Beach, Signal Hill) District in Southern California.

"I credit my campaign success to a large number of fine volunteers in the primary who made over 37,000 telephone calls in my favor," Bond told us in his capitol office.

Republican Bond was underfinanced in the primary: he spent only $17,000 against his opponent's $39,000. This was his first try for election, and in the finals, his party was outnumbered in registration by 20 per cent.

Bond had majored in political science at Stanford, where he was an All-American basketball player. As administrator of housing rehabilitation, he had built one of the first model cities. He had a clean record of thirteen years in personnel, administrative, and community improvement in Los Angeles county.

But Bill Bond had spent all of his working time in downtown Los Angeles, and it was vital that he become known within the district in which he wished to serve.

It helped that he had been a high school All-American at St. Anthony's in Long Beach. That gave him some local name recognition, but not enough to win an election.

With the help of Clint Engledow, another campaign neophyte who later became Bond's administrative assistant, Bond formed a volunteer corps that eventually gave his qualifications over the phone to an additional 21,000 following his primary victory. They also recruited a crew that knocked on almost 50,000 doors the last five days of the campaign.

The results: Bill Bond the winner by 8,000 votes!

"Now, if you don't think it takes good volunteers. . . ." Bond smiled at us. "You've got to have volunteers!"

Bill Bond's district was recently reapportioned, and he is temporarily out of office. But his backers say he'll be back, with another group of willing volunteers showing the way.

Campaign Insight is filled with interesting short stories on "how to" win elections:

Political novice Helen Sommers overcame a tough identity problem to win a seat in the Washington state legislature with 52.2 per cent of the vote. She made use of computer analyses, door-to-door work, direct mail, speaking engagements, and coffee gatherings.

Robert M. Crisler, a geographer at the University of Southwestern Louisiana in Lafayette, knocked on 85 per cent of the 45th representative district's doors to meet face-to-face with the people he wanted to serve in the legislature. A necessity brought about by lack of funds, ". . . became an electoral asset," Crisler told *Campaign Insight.* "In a district as small as my own, shoe leather can defeat money."

Phil Bladine didn't win his nomination in the 1974 congressional primary, but his volunteer delegates from hometown McMinnville, Oregon, will never forget *Bladine's Barnstorming Bus,* and the impact this small-town group made as they traveled in air-conditioned forty-passenger chartered buses in a series of trips over Oregon's highways and winding country roads passing out campaign literature and conviviality.

If nothing else, Bladine's volunteers proved there can be fun in losing.

One small-town bus excursion that didn't lose was in the "Clare Berryhill for Senator" campaign.

Calling on his most tangible asset—his family—Berryhill, an independent San Joaquin Valley rancher who produces grapes, almonds, and cattle, covered California's extensive Third Senatorial District in a large motor home.

"We painted it up fancy," Berryhill told us in an interview in his capitol office. "We put a big sign—JOIN THE BERRY-HILL BANDWAGON—on each side."

Then Berryhill, his wife, Maryellen, and their five active children traversed the Sierra Nevada from Yosemite to the Oregon border. On a series of jaunts starting from their Ceres ranch home, they were determined to shake every hand, walk every street, and knock on every door in the far-flung district.

"We made every county fair," Clare Berryhill proudly remembers. "We had a little brass band, my kids and some of their friends. We'd give out with the music and crowds would gather. Between sets, we talked about agricultural problems and free enterprise and strong local government. We blew up free balloons. . . ."

In eight months of intermittent traveling through the rugged terrain, the Berryhills logged over 60,000 miles. They proved that sometimes it isn't the big city professionals who know all the answers about campaigning.

For you to do now:
Seek out an elective office that needs someone special to fill the job.
It may be you!
If you're not the one for the position, find someone who is.
Work for his or her election, night and day!

Chapter
14. LOBBYISTS

The lobbyist!

You visualize him as a grossly fat individual, with heavy lips closing around a smoldering cigar stub, his diamond-encrusted pudgy fingers holding packs of high-denomination currency, with more dollars—labeled "big business"—cascading from overloaded pockets.

His seedy-looking companion is "the legislator," who reaches with greedy hands to grab what he can while he has a chance.

Right?

Not so!

Not from all we've learned about what is more formally referred to as "the legislative advocate."

A little research will show you that today's lobbyist could well be a clubwoman from Iowa. Or a young college grad from Tennessee. Or a high school teacher from Georgia, or Texas, or upstate New York.

Harmon Zeigler, in his book *Interest Groups in American Society,* wrote:

> A brief visit to Washington would be enough to persuade most students of politics that many lobbyists are not very powerful and menacing at all; that they are in fact more dependent upon the good will of elected politicians than the reverse.

171

Not that the original stereotype wasn't an earned one.

Huge oil interests, railroads, sugar companies, the brewing and distilling industries, manufacturers of all types, trucking, banking, insurance, racing (horse and dog), labor —in short, any endeavors that stood to make an extra dollar with the help of local, state, and national government have long had representation where it did the most good: close to the policymakers.

The term "lobby" comes from mid-seventeenth century England where men called "lobby-agents" approached members of Parliament in an anteroom close by the floor of the House of Commons.

In early nineteenth century literature, the American usage of the term was introduced by Dennis Tilden Lynch, who wrote about corruption in the New York statehouse: "Corruption has erected her court on the heights of the Hudson, in the avenues of Albany, in the lobby of the legislature . . . Her throne was the lobby."

Men bent on influencing votes in favor of their clients gathered about the vestibules of Congress and literally cornered the members on their way into chambers, forcing their issues on the makers of policy.

When it was discovered that a more subtle approach could be made over fine wine and the tasty victuals of the era, lobbying became more and more sophisticated.

Sophisticated, and at the same time uninhibited, until finally, in 1890, when the Massachusetts Anti-lobbying Act was adopted, it was outlawed, or at least controlled in Massachusetts.

Antilobbying bills passed the United States Senate in 1928 and 1935, but failed in the House. In 1946 the Regulation of Lobbying Act became law, and it became necessary for lobbyists to register in Washington.

Of all the lobbyists who have practiced that "art," perhaps

the best known is a figure unfamiliar on Washington's Capitol Hill.

The dubious distinction of being named the country's most notorious legislative advocate belongs to the late Arthur H. Samish, who literally ran the California legislature to suit his and his clients' needs.

Artie Samish's power was unmistakable.

So was his audacity.

When he was once asked by a newspaper reporter how he was getting along with the governor, Samish answered, "I am the governor of the legislature. To hell with the Governor of California."

His brazen way with the press got him national recognition in 1949 when Carey McWilliams wrote in *The Nation*: "Although Samish is known to everyone in California who is directly interested in politics, I would venture to guess that not one percent of the voters could identify his name, although he is, beyond all doubt, the political boss of the State."

Working from a suite on the fourth floor of the Senator Hotel, across "L" Street from the Capitol, Artie Samish "selected and elected" assemblymen and senators, and had them defeated when they didn't vote according to his dictums. He had mayors and United States congressmen elected, and delivered the California delegation to a presidential candidate—Republican Wendell Willkie.

California's Earl Warren, who was later to become chief justice of the United States Supreme Court, when being interviewed by Lester Velie for a 1949 *Collier's* magazine article, was asked, "Who has more influence with the legislature, you or Artie Samish?"

Governor Warren answered candidly, "On matters that affect his clients, Artie unquestionably has more power than the governor."

The Secret Boss of California—the title of the Velie article, as well as of a Samish autobiography written with Bob Thomas—did his particular brand of legislative magic from 1930 until 1955; then he went to McNeil Island Federal Penitentiary for income tax violations.

A man of huge proportions—six feet, two inches tall, 300 pounds—Artie was not without a sense of humor as he showed his disdain for the legislators of the day. When Velie asked for a photo session, Samish brought out a ventriloquist's dummy, plopped it on his knee, and said, "That's the way I lobby. That's my legislature. That's Mr. Legislature. *How are you today, Mr. Legislature?*"

And Artie Samish proceeded to manipulate the dummy as easily as he did the men in chambers on the other side of "L" Street.

In his book, Samish recounted his words, given to Lester Velie:

> There was only one way the [lobby] situation would change. I gave the secret in the last paragraph of the *Collier's* articles. Velie asked me how the people of California could get rid of me and people like me.
> "There is one way," I told him. "The people must take more interest in the men they elect."
> As long as the people of California paid only $1,200 a year to the men who made their laws, as long as most candidates were elected in the primaries, as long as most citizens didn't even know the names of their Senators and Assemblymen, then the people would not get rid of Art Samish.

There have been many changes in the California capital since Samish's heydey. Cross-filing, to which Samish referred when speaking of electing candidates in the primaries, has been repealed. Legislators now receive a salary of $23,230, plus a per diem expense account of $30.00, a gasoline credit card, and a state-leased automobile.

Their office suites are more spacious, their staffs larger

and more knowledgeable, and research facilities more complete.

And in 1974, lobby laws that would have caused Artie Samish to groan with anguish were passed.

Prop 9, the initiative measure approved by the voters in the election of that year, gave birth to the Fair Political Practices Commission, through the Political Reform Act. The act forbids lobbyists to make political contributions, and limits spending to ten dollars per month for the benefit of any one legislator.

In Samish's time, when daily noon buffets included lobster, canapes, the finest wines and liquors, and only the best Scotch whiskey, a legislator could easily down enough luncheon goodies to make a ten-dollar monthly minimum appear like a cheap tip to the Senator Hotel's bell captain.

All this is a thing of the past. Fred Taugher, consultant to the Assembly Rules Committee, has announced that the free doughnuts, orange juice, milk, coffee, and ice cream bars, all provided by industries with a legislative axe to grind, would have to be charged to the lawmakers.

Senate President Pro Tem James R. Mills also came up with the sad news that lobbyists would no longer serve late afternoon snacks of cheese and crackers, cold cuts and rye bread.

The squirrels that run beneath the arching trees of Capitol Park have felt the weight of the new law, too.

Eugene Chappie, a Roseville Republican assemblyman, whose walnut-growing constituents had supplied him with nuts for the animals, said he could no longer accept them as a gratuity. Instead, he hoped to receive one dollar from each legislator to purchase the snacks for his furry friends.

Not all legislative advocates view the new law with dismay. While some lobbyists who previously had spent as much as $3,000 a month in Sacramento bars and restaurants during busy legislative periods were having much trouble filling out the necessary forms and interpreting the rules, the Women's Christian Temperance Union experienced no problems. Their lobbyist, David A. Depew, reported $110 for total January expenses, including air fares, $25 for lobbyist registration fees, and a few miscellaneous items.

Success in curtailing lobby abuses in California has little direct relation with the Washington lobby.

The Federal Regulation of Lobbying Act, a statute since 1946, has been vilified by influence groups and Congress alike, from the day its constitutionality was upheld in a landmark case by Supreme Court Chief Justice Earl Warren.

The First Amendment to the Constitution reads, in part:

> Congress shall make no law . . . abridging the freedom of speech, or the press; or the right of people peaceably to assemble, and to petition Government for a redress of grievances.

It is in this amendment that all lobbyists seek refuge. But the law requires paid lobbyists to register with the clerk of the House and the secretary of the Senate, and to file quarterly financial reports with the House clerk. It doesn't curtail their activities.

Section 307 of the act reads:

> The provisions . . . shall apply to any person . . . who by himself, or through any agent or employee or other persons . . . solicits, collects, or receives money or any other thing of value to be used principally to aid in . . .
> a.) The passage or defeat of any legislation by the Congress of the United States.
> b.) To influence, directly or indirectly, the passage or defeat of any legislation by the Congress of the United States.

The late President John F. Kennedy, when he was still a Democratic senator from Massachusetts, had a much quoted realistic view of the legislative advocate:

Lobbyists are in many cases expert technicians and capable of explaining complex and difficult subjects in a clear and understandable fashion.

Lobbyists prepare briefs, memorandums, legislative analyses, and draft legislation for use by committees and Members of Congress; they are necessarily masters of their subject and, in fact, they frequently can provide useful statistics and information not otherwise available. . . .

The Kennedy concept describes the lobbyist at his or her most valuable posture in contributing to government. It ignores the role of the legislative advocate as influence peddler.

It may be true that the Washington lobby has its fair share of experts among its practitioners. However, it is well known that the elite member of the lobbyist group is the lawyer.

It is generally accepted, too, that most lawyers have no expertise with regard to how pulp wood is turned into paper, how collapsible bumpers can be attached to compact cars, or how the safflower thistle can be turned into lubricating oil.

Congress itself shows a majority of lawyers in its makeup: 54 per cent—289 members in 1973—had passed the bar exams.

Other lawyers who have worked as congressional staff, or among the executive branch liaison, or as departmental deputies, have used the experience gained on The Hill or within the White House complex to further their usefulness as lobbyists.

One of these, Charls E. Walker, parlayed his intimate knowledge of the administration, gathered during twenty years in Washington politics, to start his own firm in 1973, Charls E. Walker Associates, Inc.

Within six months of incorporation, Walker's company had corralled fourteen major corporations as clients, twelve of them ranked in the top ninety of the nation's and the world's economic leaders, according to a profile in *The Washington Lobby*.

With all the lobby-lawyers and congressional-lawyers in the nation's capital, it was only a fulfillment of a natural law that another lawyer came on the scene to fill a vacuum.

His name is Ralph Nader.

At present the best authority on Ralph Nader is Robert F. Buckhorn.

In his book, *Nader, the People's Lawyer*, Buckhorn has drawn the most complete portrait possible of this very private publicly committed man.

Intensive interviews with Nader, traveling around the country with him, conducting over two hundred interviews with people close to or acquainted with him at one time or another in his busy life—people ranging from his mother, Mrs. Rose Nader, to his antagonist, General Motors board chairman James Roche—all have combined to give Buckhorn insight into the founder of "Nader's Raiders."

A voracious reader and prolific writer, Nader was a Phi Beta Kappa at Princeton and graduated magna cum laude in 1955. His Harvard Law School experience was highlighted more by his writing than his search for academic honors. As an editor of the *Record*, he learned the value of the press as a means of communicating and expressing his theories.

His early magazine articles in *The Nation* and the *New Republic* gave Nader his most effective forum, according to Buckhorn. Writings for such exposes as "fat dogs" and "shamburgers," x-rays, job safety, coalminer's black lung disease, filthy fish, and "The Infernal, Eternal, Internal Combustion Engine" in the *New Republic* were "usually timed to coincide with an upcoming Congressional hearing or to spark a wave of newspaper stories on an issue Nader felt was being ignored" Buckhorn related.

Beginning with his Center for Study of Responsive Law, in May, 1969, Nader has caused no less than ten separate enterprises to come into being, all of them designed to give industry, the corporate lobby, and Congress a conglomerate headache.

The center, which was begun partly with the proceeds from Nader's best-selling book, *Unsafe at Any Speed,* first published in 1965, started as a typical Nader dream.

"The concept jelled in his mind as far back as his college days," wrote Buckhorn. "He saw then a need for what would be basically a think tank for consumers; a place where consumer-minded lawyers, engineers, and scientists would research, write, and evolve policies and strategies."

Between 1969 and 1971, the Raiders filed reports on nineteen areas of public and consumer interest, including the Federal Trade Commission, interstate commerce, food and drugs, water and air pollution, occupational safety and health, old age, aviation, antitrust enforcement, and the medical profession, to name a few.

Most of these choice studies were made in the face of a glowering Washington lobby, all still waiting for Ralph Nader to make the mistake that will begin his rapid decline. The consensus is that the flaw may be found in his proliferation, spreading himself too thin, expanding his plan to include areas where not even he can cover all bases.

Of the other enterprises created, backed, and advised by Nader which his adversaries hope will prove his undoing is the Public Interest Research Group (PIRG, pronounced, conveniently, "the purge"). The PIRG is second in size to the Center for Study of Responsive Law.

Begun in June, 1971, the PIRG is composed of a small staff of attorneys who are willing to dedicate part of their careers—on one year contracts—at $4,500-per-year salaries.

"Bright, top-of-their-class talent," Buckhorn described them, "the PIRG lawyers pound the halls of Congress, mak-

ing contact with the young Congressional aides and committee counsels. Not registered as lobbyists, the PIRG lawyers cannot go directly to the Congressmen and Senators,
but the web they have spun over Congressional staffers is a
tribute to their fast growing expertise in the ways of politics."

The PIRG involves itself with such major assignments as
the nation's system of property tax assessment, transportation, and deceptive advertising in drugs.

Nader's running battle with General Motors, GMC trucks,
and the Corvair (subject of *Unsafe at Any Speed*) is
handled through the PIRG. Nader received some satisfaction during the course of this historic dispute when GM
paid him $425,000 in an out-of-court settlement for his $7
million invasion-of-privacy suit in 1970.

The Center for Auto Safety and its two spin-offs—the
Center for Concerned Engineering and Professionals for
Auto Safety—cover this vital field in consumer interest.

The Aviation Consumer Action Project works toward
"passenger power." The Health Research Group explores
the world of medicine. The Corporate Accountability Research Group hopes to fight political interference in antitrust cases.

On through a long list of consumer-oriented problems
with manufacturers, with government, and with the law,
Ralph Nader has worked tirelessly, living alone in a room-
inghouse, and existing on the salary he pays his PIRGers,
less than $5,000 a year, plus his traveling expenses. All of
his income, and it comes to well over six figures, goes into
his many projects.

In recent years, more than ever before, legislative advocates
are entering the political action on the side of the taxpayer
and consumer.

Common Cause—"the citizens' lobby"—began in 1970;

founder John W. Gardner is still its chairman, and Jack T. Conway is its current president.

With a fast growth rate which subsided somewhat in 1972, then boomed again in 1974, Common Cause boasts of 323,000 dues-paying members at $15 apiece who made it possible for the organization to be top spender of all organizations filing lobby reports in 1973. The total spent was $934,835.

During 1973 and 1974 Common Cause set as its priority campaign spending and financing reform, intent on breaking the hold of the influence-buyers through a public financing system.

In reporting that only 84 of the 435 persons elected to the House failed to respond to key reform questions, Common Cause said, "We think that shows conclusively that the momentum is with reform in 1975."

Before Common Cause, and even before Ralph Nader opened his first center, a Los Angeles automobile salesman named Ed Koupal sat in his kitchen with his wife, Joyce, and his three daughters. It was 1967. They were unhappy with the new California governor, Ronald Reagan, and they didn't know what to do about it.

The Koupals mulled over their frustration, and finally decided to start a recall petition.

Their recall failed, as did other attempts to oust the governor that followed.

But it was the beginning of the People's Lobby, which was founded with 20,000 members in 1969, most of whom were among those who had signed the first "Recall Reagan" petition.

The People's Lobby found some success when they backed Proposition 20 in the 1972 election. This led to the Coastal Zone Conservation Act which closed California's diminishing coastline to indiscriminate building, and established a method of preservation, protection, restoration, and enhancement of the ecology and coastal environment.

The true strength of the People's Lobby showed in the 1974 elections, however, when they backed the now famous "Prop 9," the Political Reform Initiative.

It was the Koupal's use of the initiative process that drew Judi Phillips into their People's Lobby—all the way.

"I saw they were doing something about the environment three years ago," Judi told us. "They were really taking action. It was a moving group and I got very excited with it."

Judi, working out of *her* home—the Koupals still work out of theirs—is now a full-time lobbyist in Sacramento.

"We try to work through the legislative process," she stated. "I've noticed a great change in the legislature toward People's Lobby since we passed the political reform proposition. Before that, the legislators automatically voted down anything I said I was for. Now, since Prop 9 has passed, they listen. I've testified on two bills recently, and they passed both of them out of committee."

Judi paused for affect, savoring her words, enjoying her moment of triumph.

"They have a *fear* of us!" she grinned.

Judi is a small, almost fragile appearing brunette. But strength shines in her eyes.

"They don't listen to us because they like us," she said of the legislature. "We lobby through pressure. We embarrass them publicly. We go in and sue them if they're not doing something correctly under the campaign disclosure laws. We're very loud about what we're doing, but we have a way of doing things without them—by that, I mean the initiative. This gives us our power."

The People's Lobby is currently concentrating on a nationwide drive for a proposed Initiative and Vote of Confidence amendment to the Constitution—the twenty-seventh, if all goes well with their plan.

National Initiative

The people of the United States of America reserve for themselves the power of the initiative. The initiative is the power of the electors to propose laws and to adopt or reject them. An initiative measure may not be submitted to alter or amend the Constitution of the United States.

Vote of Confidence
(Recall)

Every elected officer of the United States may be removed from office at any time by the electors meeting the qualifications to vote in his State through the procedure and in the manner herein provided for, which procedure shall be known as a vote of confidence, and is in addition to any other method of removal provided by law.

We asked if the People's Lobby citizen-workers were all volunteers.

"Most of them are volunteers," Judi Phillips told us. "Several of us who work full time are on salary. I'm the highest paid. I get $300 per month."

That leaves a wide choice of careers for budding lobbyists:

You can make a lot of money.

Or you can make just a little.

Or—and you've heard this before—you can be a volunteer.

For you to do now:

Read *The Washington Lobby*. (It should be in your local library.)

Investigate and join a citizens' lobby.

Chapter

15. ETHICS IN ELECTIVE GOVERNMENT

Something has to be right with a nation that can hold itself together, however tenuously at times, through 200 years of trial and triumph, poor judgment and good, wars (just and unjust), economic imbalance, racial altercation, and every kind of tactical, social, and political error imaginable.

Brow-holders and breast-beaters have throughout the history of the United States castigated "them" for "their" lack of high ethical standards as "they" went on their destructive way bringing the republic to utter and inevitable chaos.

"They" were around when the Constitution was formed, and they will be among us when the next century rolls around.

They are, of course, those with whom we do not agree.

"There are two Americas," wrote Senator J. William Fulbright in *The Arrogance of Power*.

One is the America of Lincoln and Adlai Stevenson; the other the America of Teddy Roosevelt and the modern superpatriots. One is generous and humane, the other narrowly egotistical; one is self-critical, the other self-righteous; one is sensible, the other romantic; one is good-humored, the other solemn; one is enquiring, the other pontificating; one is moderate, the other filled with passionate intensity; one is judicious and the other arrogant in the use of great power.

And America, says the senator from Arkansas, seems to be able to show both faces on occasion at the same time.

Fulbright was also intrigued by our dual humanism-puritanism:

> Throughout our history two strands have coexisted uneasily—a dominant strand of democratic humanism and a lesser but durable strand of intolerant puritanism. There has been a tendency through the years for reason and moderation to prevail as long as things are going tolerably well or as long as our problems seem clear and finite and manageable. But when things have gone badly for any length of time, or when the reasons for adversity have seemed obscure, or simply when some event or leader of opinion has aroused the people to a state of high emotion, our puritan spirit has tended to break through, leading us to look at the world through the distorting prism of a harsh and angry moralism.

Who are these citizens who can afford the luxury of harsh and angry moralism?

Are they the people working within government? The activists? The members of people's lobbies? The youth groups? The party workers? The volunteeers for all causes?

Chances are *they* are represented among those mentioned.

The Census Bureau says that of 141,000,000 persons eligible to vote in November, 1974, 53,000,000 failed to even register.

Do those 53,000,000 feel so morally angry that they refuse to partake in the one exercise that could give them the freedom so fervently desired?

Or is this nonregistering, nonvoting posture a cheap cop-out?

In past generations—with some holdovers into the present—it was not considered "nice" to discuss religion or politics except among an esoteric few.

Was this brought on by a high moral ethic?

Or was it brought about by the same syndrome that led over 50 million potential voters away from the registration books?

Was it the same cop-out?

Or was it simply ignorance of the facts about elective government and those who reach the power plateau?

Complaints about unresponsive representation in city hall, in state capitols, and in Washington are so commonplace as to lose all credence because of repetition and poor presentation.

Unless one knows how the system is designed, it is often difficult at best to try to make sense out of a puzzle that can be easily solved with a little beforehand knowledge.

Dr. Charles J. Zinn, in *How Our Laws Are Made*, a government document (No. 920323) prepared for the general information of the public, makes a patient plea for understanding in this regard:

> The Federal legislative process is ordinarily a lengthy and somewhat complex one that is often the butt of ridicule by the uninformed and by those who seek to undermine our Constitutional way of life. On the one hand, complaints are heard about "the law's delays" both with regard to the administration of justice by our courts and the enactments of laws by the Congress. On the other hand, it is not uncommon for the same individuals to charge that a particular bill has been "steamrollered" through the Congress.
>
> Manifestly, no system of enacting laws to govern more than 200 million persons can be perfect in all its details with respect to every single piece of legislation.
>
> However, by and large, neither of these complaints is justified and, discounting the sly but vicious attacks by hostile persons or groups that often make dupes of otherwise well intentioned persons, the invective against our deliberate lawmaking procedure is quite likely to stem from a fundamental lack of information and understanding regarding that procedure.

Knowledge is the purest ethic.

Involvement leads to knowledge.

Of the 12 million potential voters in the 18-20-year-old group, only about one in five bothered to vote.

Why? Out of ignorance? Because of listening to the sly, vicious, hostile persons about whom Dr. Zinn wrote?

It's a hard choice to make:

> I didn't vote because I'm ignorant of the system.
> I didn't vote because I was duped.

Of course, there are the lazy.

> I didn't vote because I was too lazy to become informed.

Or,

> I didn't vote because I just don't care.

During the course of our study on all the aspects of elective government, we asked young people who had become deeply involved with internships, volunteer work, and party politics what their reaction was, and the reaction of their peer group when they returned to campus or to high school. Invariably, it followed these lines:

"I feel I have grown away from my friends, somehow. At first that bothered me. But I have made so many more new friends, who have so much more to offer, so many more things to talk about."

One young graduate, just entering law school after a stint as a legislative intern, said, "I live in this small community where everyone knows everyone else. I was really looking forward to going home, to sharing my experiences about my year in government. But there was no one to share them with. They just didn't speak my language anymore.

They seemed so remote from what's going on in the real world. And they didn't seem to want to do anything about it."

Another person, a college student lobbyist/intern/organizer for Young Americans for Freedom, told us, "The trouble with our work is getting people who want to become involved."

Involvement. Knowledge.

There is no secret in the fact that some of our elected officials have been lacking in high moral standards. Should this act as a depressing agent, discouraging us from further participation in the system?

Not according to Herbert Kaufman, who feels the future will test us in our capacity to meet its challenges, with no automatic victories assured. Dr. Kaufman sees the situation as a continuous battle, but one which should exhilarate us.

"The situation should not be cause for pessimism," he says, "but for excitement, and even for gratification, because to continue fighting these battles is to remain free."

The question is how to fight the battle.

A major source of communication in recent years has been found in so-called "talk radio," where listeners telephone in and discuss, pro and con, all manner of subjects and problems of the day.

One of these shows, *The Jim Eason Show*, broadcast from KGO, San Francisco, featured Cal-Berkeley professor Ralph Goldman, who was attempting to inform the listeners and callers-in on how the system works.

"People have wishes," Goldman said, "and have liberal or conservative orientation, and are so attached to these wishes that they fail to understand how they should skillfully manipulate this system so they can get more of what they want, rather than less."

The basic ignorance of so many of the callers-in about how government works was apparent to anyone who had done even the least rudimentary research on the subject; to Dr. Goldman it was astounding.

Carefully he explained how to bring a problem to the attention of a congressman or a state assemblyman:

Be sure of your stand.
Be articulate.
Don't threaten.
Bring your problem forth on an "even keel"—be cool.
On closing, however, say: "If you don't pay more attention to us and our problem, we will remember this on election day." Politely!

But, Dr. Goldman explained, be sure your new candidate is viable. Certain types of candidates just aren't going to make it. "You have to figure out how to get at least some of your views accepted by the majority with whom you have to negotiate."

This advice is true at the village level, municipal level, state level, and Washington level. And it holds for any ideology or philosophy to which you adhere.

It is necessary to become informed on every aspect of whatever views you hold—left, right, or middle.

An informed electorate will demand a high morality in government. An informed electorate will control power in government.

"Freedom rests on ethical decisions," says Peter F. Drucker in *The Future of Industrial Man.* "But the political sphere deals with power. And power is only a tool and in itself ethically neutral. It is not a social purpose and not an ethical principle."

However, power under control can serve highly ethical social purposes.

Technologically speaking, socially speaking, politically speaking, it's a new world we face going into the future. Margaret

Mead, noted anthropologist, speaking to the graduating class of Simmons College, Boston, 1975, brought out these points, and called for a reevaluation in this country of our whole position regarding energy, consumption of resources, and finances. Her closing remarks seem pertinent here:

> And so we have to learn something new, and it's going to be rough. But you are the ones that have to ask the questions, you are the ones that have come in with fresh eyes, most of you haven't tried to live with total responsibility in this world and so you're going to have a chance to look at the situation fresh while the older people in it are doing our best to readjust our sights, to reassess the hopes we had, to realize that we have to change the way in which we are building life up, change it very radically and very responsibly and that it's possible.

Change is possible.
Ethical change is a necessity.
"The best way to change things in America is through the political process," former Oklahoma Senator Fred Harris, a Democratic candidate for the presidency told us at the California convention. "Our very best people should be involved in it."
Doesn't this mean you?

For you to do now:
  Become aware.
  Get involved!

A SELECTED DIRECTORY OF PUBLIC SERVICE INTERNSHIPS

Opportunities for the High School, Undergraduate, Graduate, and Postgraduate Student.

This selected directory has been compiled to assist the student in applying for a public service internship or fellowship program within his or her immediate locale, although the scope of recruitment is nationwide in many programs. Municipal, state, and federal programs are included. To receive complete information on each program listed, it will be necessary for the student or instructor/counselor to communicate directly with the institution or agency listed.

However, programs marked (1) have been outlined in a directory distributed by the National Center for Public Service Internship Programs; those programs marked (2) have been outlined in a Supplement to *Who Administers?* by Frank Logue. Information on these two publications is included in a separate bibliography of related publications (page 203) following this selected directory. The outlines include: objectives and designs of programs; scope of recruitment and placement; screening and selection procedures; admission requirements; remuneration and stipends; and obligations upon completion of the programs.

ATLANTA FELLOWS & INTERNS PROGRAM (1)
Atlanta University Center
360 Westview Drive, S.W.
Atlanta, Georgia 30310
(404) 522-8881

ATLANTA URBAN CORPS (1)
Georgia State University
University Plaza
Atlanta, Georgia 30303
(404) 658-3558

BUSH LEADERSHIP FELLOWS PROGRAM (1)(2)
P.O. Box 15125
Minneapolis, Minnesota 55415
(612) 227-0891 St. Paul
(612) 926-0948 Minneapolis

CALIFORNIA ASSEMBLY INTERNSHIP PROGRAM
    (1)(2)
Assembly, P.O. Box 91, State Capitol
Sacramento, California 95814
(916) 445-6781

CALIFORNIA GOVERNMENT INTERNSHIP
    PROGRAM (2)
California State University at Fullerton
800 North State College Boulevard
Fullerton, California
(714) 870-2115

CALIFORNIA SENATE INTERNSHIP PROGRAMS
Senate Internship Selection Panel
State Capitol, Room 2052
Sacramento, California 95814
(916) 445-9463

CALIFORNIA UCLA GOVERNMENT INTERNSHIP
    PROGRAM (2)
University of California at Los Angeles
161 Kerckhoff Hall, 405 Hilgard Avenue
Los Angeles, California 90024
(213) 825-7041

CONGRESSIONAL FELLOWSHIP PROGRAM (1)
1527 New Hampshire Avenue, N.W.
Washington, D. C. 20036
(202) 483-2512

CONGRESSIONAL INTERNSHIPS IN TECHNOLOGY
   ASSESSMENT (1)
Stanford University
Stanford, California 94305
(415) 497-3080 or 497-4169

CONGRESSIONAL SCIENCE AND ENGINEERING
   FELLOW PROGRAM (1)
The American Association for the Advancement of Science
1515 Massachusetts Avenue, N.W.
Washington, D.C. 20005
(202) 467-4475

CONNECTICUT GENERAL ASSEMBLY INTERN
   PROGRAM (1) (2)
Office of Legislative Research
Room 120, State Capitol
Hartford, Connecticut 06115
(203) 566-4150

CORO FOUNDATION FELLOWS PROGRAM:
   INTERNSHIPS IN PUBLIC AFFAIRS (1) (2)
Coro Foundation
215 West Fifth Street
Los Angeles, California 90013
(212) 623-1234

Coro Foundation
149 Ninth Street
San Francisco, California 94103
(415) 863-4601

Coro Foundation
4378 Lindell Boulevard
St. Louis, Missouri 63108
(314) 534-5100

DOL-MAP MANPOWER INTERN TRAINING
    PROGRAM (2)
1025 Connecticut Avenue, N.W.
Washington, D. C. 20036
(202) 296-1312

FORD LEADERSHIP DEVELOPMENT PROGRAM
    (SOUTHWEST) (2)
809 First National Bank Building, East
5301 Central Avenue, N. E.
Albuquerque, New Mexico 87108
(505) 256-2850

FORD LEADERSHIP DEVELOPMENT PROGRAM
    (REGION-AT-LARGE) (2)
12566 West 38th Avenue
Wheatridge, Colorado 80033
(303) 422-6121

FORD LEADERSHIP DEVELOPMENT PROGRAM
    (NORTHEAST REGION) (2)
24 Broadway
Farmington, Maine 04938
(207) 778-3386

GEORGIA INTERN PROGRAM (2)
State Capitol
Atlanta, Georgia 30334
(404) 656-1794

HAWAII STATE LEGISLATIVE INTERN PROGRAM;
    HAWAII STATE EXECUTIVE CITY & COUNTY OF
    HONOLULU ADMINISTRATIVE INTERN
    PROGRAM (1)
Center for Governmental Development
1394 A Lower Campus Drive
Honolulu, Hawaii 96822

HEW FELLOWS PROGRAM (2)
330 Independence Avenue, S. W. Room 5309 N.
Washington, D. C. 20201
(202) 962-4989

HUD URBAN INTERN PROGRAM (1) (2)
451 7th Street, S.W.
Washington, D. C. 20410
(202) 755-5492

IDAHO GOVERNOR'S SUMMER INTERN PROGRAM
(1)
Director, Department of Administration
145 Len B. Jordan Building
Boise, Idaho 83720
(208) 384-3380

ILLINOIS GOVERNOR'S SUMMER FELLOWSHIP
PROGRAM (1)
Governor's Office
State of Illinois
Springfield, Illinois 62706
(217) 782-5160

ILLINOIS GRADUATE PUBLIC SERVICE
INTERNSHIP (1)
Sangamon State University
Springfield, Illinois 62708
(217) 786-6750

ILLINOIS LEGISLATIVE STAFF INTERNSHIP
PROGRAM (1) (2)
Sangamon State University
Springfield, Illinois 62708
(217) 786-6611

ILLINOIS SUMMER FELLOWSHIPS IN
    STATE GOVERNMENT (2)
Governor's Office
State House
Springfield, Illinois 62706
(217) 525-2239

IOWA STATE OFFICE FOR PLANNING & PROGRAM-
    MING; STATE PLANNING INTERNSHIPS (1)
523 East 12th Street
Des Moines, Iowa 50312

KANSAS MASTERS OF PUBLIC ADMINISTRATION (2)
510 Blake Hall
University of Kansas
Lawrence, Kansas 66044
(913) UN 4-3523

KENTUCKY—FRANKFORT ADMINISTRATIVE
    INTERN PROGRAM (2)
Room 106, 309 Shelby Street
Frankfort, Kentucky 40601
(502) 564-4881

KENTUCKY—FRANKFORT LEGISLATIVE INTERN
    PROGRAM (2)
Room 106, 309 Shelby Street
Frankfort, Kentucky 40601
(502) 564-4881

MASSACHUSETTS PUBLIC SERVICE INTERN
    PROGRAM (2)
141 Milk Street
Boston, Massachusetts 02109
(617) 727-4088

MICHIGAN GOVERNMENT INTERNSHIP
 PROGRAM (1)
Michigan Department of Civil Service
Lewis Cass Building
320 South Walnut Street
Lansing, Michigan 48913
(517) 373-2664

MINNESOTA GOVERNOR'S INTERNSHIP
 PROGRAM (1)
215 Administration Building
St. Paul, Minnesota 55155
(612) 296-2329

MINORITIES IN CITY GOVERNMENT (1) (2)
1140 Connecticut Avenue, N.W.
Washington, D.C. 20036
(202) 293-2200

MISSOURI MODEL COMMITTEE STAFF PROJECT IN
 HEALTH (MCSP) INTERN PROGRAM (1)
Citizens Conference on State Legislatures
4722 Broadway
Kansas City, Missouri 64112
(816) 531-8104

NASPAA PUBLIC ADMINISTRATION FELLOWS
 PROGRAM (1) (2)
1220 Connecticut Avenue, N.W.
Washington, D.C. 20036
(202) 785-3260

NATIONAL URBAN FELLOWS (1) (2)
P.O. Box 1475
New Haven, Connecticut 06506
(203) 624-5168

NEW JERSEY GOVERNMENTS CAREER INTERNSHIP
    PROGRAM (1)
c/o Public Service Institute
Route One at Emmons Drive
Princeton, New Jersey 08540

NEW JERSEY INTERNS IN PUBLIC SERVICE (1) (2)
New Jersey Department of Community Affairs
P.O. Box 2768
Trenton, New Jersey 08625
(609) 292-6192

NEW YORK CITY URBAN FELLOWSHIP PROGRAM
    (1) (2)
Mayor's Office of Administration
250 Broadway, 14th floor
New York, New York 10007
(212) 566-1216

NEW YORK PUBLIC ADMINISTRATION INTERNSHIP
    PROGRAM (2)
1220 Washington Avenue
Albany, New York 12226
(518) 457-4292

NEW YORK PUBLIC ADMINISTRATION PROGRAMS
    (2)
Syracuse University
211 Maxwell
Syracuse, New York 13210
(315) 476-5541, ext. 4296

NEW YORK STATE ASSEMBLY INTERN PROGRAM (1)
Legislative Office Building, 834
Albany, New York 12224
(518) 472-6648

NEW YORK STATE LEGISLATIVE INTERNSHIP
PROGRAM (1)
Comparative Development Studies Center
Mohawk 1210
State University of New York at Albany
Albany, New York 12222
(518) 457-3300

NORTH CAROLINA SERVICE LEARNING PROGRAM
IN COMMUNITY EDUCATION (2)
University of North Carolina at Charlotte
UNCC Station
Charlotte, North Carolina 28213
(704) 596-5970, ext. 307

NORTH DAKOTA LEGISLATIVE INTERNSHIP
PROGRAM (1) (2)
North Dakota Legislative Council
State Capitol
Bismarck, North Dakota 58505
(701) 224-2916

OHIO AMERICAN SOCIETY FOR PUBLIC ADMINIS-
TRATION SUMMER INTERNSHIP (2)
Institute of Urban Studies
Cleveland State University
Cleveland, Ohio 44114
(216) 687-2139

OHIO LEGISLATIVE SERVICE COMMISSION
INTERNSHIP PROGRAM (1) (2)
Ohio Legislative Service Commission
Statehouse
Columbus, Ohio 43215
(614) 466-3615

OKLAHOMA STATE STUDENT GOVERNMENT
   INTERNSHIP PROGRAM (1)
Oklahoma State Regents for Higher Education
Room 118 State Capitol Building
Oklahoma City, Oklahoma 73105
(405) 521-2444

PENNSYLVANIA MASTER OF PUBLIC ADMINISTRA-
   TION (2)
Political Science Department
University of Pennsylvania
Philadelphia, Pennsylvania 19104
(215) 594-7641

PENNSYLVANIA MINORITIES IN URBAN PLANNING
   (2)
Philadelphia City Planning Commission
Penn Square
Philadelphia, Pennsylvania 19103
(215) MU 6-4619

PENNSYLVANIA, MT. LEBANON INTERNSHIP
   PROGRAM (1)
Municipal Building
710 Washington Road
Mt. Lebanon, Pennsylvania 15228
(412) 343-3400

PHOENIX MANAGEMENT INTERN PROGRAM (1)
Budget and Research Director
Municipal Building
251 West Washington, Room 821
Phoenix, Arizona 95003
(602) 262-6721

PRESIDENT'S COMMISSION ON WHITE HOUSE
   FELLOWSHIPS (1) (2)
1900 E Street, N.W., Room 1308
Washington, D.C. 20415
(202) 382-4661

RHODE ISLAND STATE GOVERNMENT INTERNSHIP
COMMISSION (1) (2)
Room 323, State House
Providence, Rhode Island 02903
(401) 277-2000

SOUTH DAKOTA LEGISLATIVE STUDENT INTERN
PROGRAM (1)
Director
Legislative Research Council
State Capitol Building
Pierre, South Dakota 57501
(605) 223-3251

SOUTH DAKOTA STUDENT INTERN PROGRAM—
EXECUTIVE BRANCH (1)
Department of Education & Cultural Affairs
State Capitol
Pierre, South Dakota 57501
(605) 224-3119

SOUTH DAKOTA UNIVERSITY COOPERATIVE FIELD
EDUCATION PROGRAM (2)
University of South Dakota
Vermillion, South Dakota 57069
(605) 677-5281

ST. LOUIS METROPOLITAN FELLOWSHIP
PROGRAM (2)
222 South Central Avenue
St. Louis, Missouri 63105
(314) 862-6200

TWIN CITY AREA URBAN CORPS (1)
1603 Chicago Avenue
Minneapolis, Minnesota 55404
(612) 348-6967

URBAN AFFAIRS INSTITUTE FELLOWSHIP
　　IN TRAINING (2)
955 Southwestern Avenue, Suite 210
Los Angeles, California 90006
(212) 737-0660

URBAN CORPS NATIONAL SERVICE CENTER (2)
1140 Connecticut Avenue, N.W., Suite 201
Washington, D.C. 20036
(202) 293-2200

URBAN MANAGEMENT PROGRAM (2)
Graduate School of Business
Stanford University
Stanford, California 94305
(415) 321-2300

UTAH STATE HOUSE FELLOWS PROGRAM (1)
118 State Capitol Building
Salt Lake City, Utah 84114
(801) 328-5245

VIRGINIA COMMONWEALTH INTERN PROGRAM (1)
State Division of Personnel
P.O. Box 654
Richmond, Virginia 23205
(804) 770-7546

WASHINGTON STATE SUMMER INTERN
　　PROGRAM (1)
Interagency Training Division
910 East 5th
Olympia, Washington 98504
(206) 753-2895

Internship Programs Designed for High School Students
EXECUTIVE HIGH SCHOOL INTERNSHIPS OF
AMERICA
680 Fifth Avenue, 9th Floor
New York, New York 10019
(212) 757-4035

PUBLICATIONS RELATED
TO INTERNSHIPS

"A Directory of Public Service Internships" (1)
The National Center for Public Service Internship Programs
Suite 601
1735 I Street, N.W.
Washington, D.C. 20006

"Who Administers?" by Frank Logue (2)
Supplement Appendix B
Access to Leadership Positions in the Administration of
    Government
The Ford Foundation
320 East 43rd Street
New York, New York 10017

"A.C.S.P. Guide to Graduate Education in Urban and
    Regional Planning"
Association of Collegiate Schools of Planning
Building 7-338
Department of Urban Studies and Planning
Massachusetts Institute of Technology
77 Massachusetts Avenue
Cambridge, Massachusetts 02139

"A Guide to Professional Development Opportunities for
    College and University Administrators"
Management Division (MD)
Academy for Educational Development
1424 Sixteenth Street, N.W.
Washington, D.C. 20036

"A Selected List of Major Fellowship Opportunities and
    Aids to Advanced Education for United States Citizens"
The Fellowship Office
Commission on Human Resources
National Research Council
Washington, D.C.

"Directory of Special Programs for Minority Group Members, 1974: Career Information Services, Employment Skills Banks, Financial Aid"
Willis L. Johnson, Editor
Garrett Park Press, Maryland 20766

"Directory of Washington Internships" (a quarterly)
National Center for Public Service Internship Programs
Suite 601
1735 I Street, N.W.
Washington, D.C. 20006

"Government Management Internships and Executive Development" by Thomas P. Murphy
Lexington Books
125 Spring Street
Lexington, Massachusetts 02173

"Graduate School Programs in Public Affairs and Public Administration, 1974"
National Association of Schools of Public Affairs and Administration (NASPAA)
1225 Connecticut Avenue, N.W. Suite 300
Washington, D.C. 20036

"National Register of Internships and Experiential Education"
Ross C. Lewchuk, editor, assisted by Richard A. Ungerer
Acropolis Books, Ltd.
Colortone Building
2400 17th Street, N.W.
Washington, D.C. 20009

"Urban Careers Guide"
National Association of Housing and Redevelopment Officials (NAHRO)
NAHRO Publications Division
2600 Virginia Avenue, N.W.
Washington, D.C. 20037

BIBLIOGRAPHY

More than 450 books are in circulation whose titles contain the phrase: *The Politics of* . . . . Countless books, texts, monographs, and pamphlets are in the libraries and at the booksellers covering the gamut of political science, government, politics, and techniques. The following list contains those publications we found useful and interesting as we wrote *Careers in Elective Government*. We recommend them to all serious students of elective self-government.

Abzug, Bella. *Bella! Ms. Abzug Goes to Washington.* Edited by Mel Ziegler. New York: Saturday Review Press, 1972.

Adams, James Truslow. *The Epic of America.* Boston: Little, Brown and Company, 1931.

Allen, Francis A. *The Crimes of Politics.* Cambridge, Mass.: Harvard University Press, 1974.

Altshuler, Alan. *City Planning Process—A Political Analysis.* Ithaca, N.Y.: Cornell University Press, 1971.

Bagley, Edward R. *Beyond the Conglomerates.* New York: AMACOM Publishers, 1974.

Baumer, William H., and Herzberg, Donald G. *Politics is Your Business.* New York: The Dial Press, 1960.

Beek, Joseph Allan. *The California Legislature.* Sacramento: California State Senate, 1960.

Bendiner, Robert. *Obstacle Course on Capitol Hill.* New York: McGraw-Hill Company, 1964.

Binkley, Wilfred E., and Moos, Malcolm, C. *A Grammar of American Politics.* New York: Alfred A. Knopf, 1949.

Brogan, D. W. *Politics in America.* New York: Harper and Brothers, 1954.

Buckhorn, Robert F. *Nader, The People's Lawyer.* Englewood Cliffs, N.J.: Prentice-Hall, Inc., 1972.

Burns, James MacGregor. *The Deadlock of Democracy.* Englewood Cliffs, N.J.: Prentice-Hall, Inc., 1963.

Caldwell, Gaylon L., and Lawrence, Robert M. *American Government Today.* New York: W. W. Norton and Company, Inc., 1963.

Careers in Politics and Political Organizations. Chicago: The Institute of Research, 1960.

Chamberlain, Hope. *A Minority of Members.* New York: Praeger Publishers, 1973.

Chambers, William, and Burnham, Walter, eds. *The American Party Systems.* New York: Oxford University Press, 1967.

Crouch, Winston W.; McHenry, Dean E.; Bollens, John C.; and Scott, Stanley. *State and Local Government in California.* Berkeley and Los Angeles: University of California Press, 1952.

Curzan, Mary H., ed. *Careers and the Study of Political Science.* Washington, D.C.: American Political Science Association, 1974.

Davidson, Roger H. *The Role of the Congressman.* New York: Pegasus, 1969.

Dexter, Lewis Anthony. *The Sociology and Politics of Congress.* Chicago: Rand McNally & Company, 1969.

Dillon, Conley H.; Leiden, Carl; and Stewart, Paul D. *Introduction to Political Science.* Van Nostrand Political Science Series. Princeton, N.J.: D. Van Nostrand, Co., Inc., 1958.

Dobrovir, William A.; Gebhardt, Joseph D.; Buffone, Samuel F.; and Oakes, Andra N. *The Offenses of Richard M. Nixon.* New York: Public Issues Press, Inc., with Quadrangle/New York Times Book Co., 1974.

Douglass, Paul, and McMahon, Alice. *How to be an Active Citizen.* Gainesville, Fla.: University of Florida Press, 1960.

Drucker, Peter F. *The Future of Industrial Man.* New York: The New American Library of the World, Inc., 1965.

Edwards, Lee. *You Can Make the Difference.* New Rochelle, N.Y.: Arlington House, 1968.

Eisenhower, Milton S. *The President is Calling*. New York: Doubleday and Company, 1974.

Fairfield, Roy, P., ed. *The Federalist Papers*. Garden City, N.Y.: Doubleday and Company, Inc., 1966.

Flathman, Richard E., and Walzer, Michael, eds. *Political Obligation*. New York: Atheneum, 1972.

Frankel, Charles. *High on Foggy Bottom*. New York: Harper and Row, 1969.

Fromkin, David. *The Question of Government*. New York: Charles Scribner's Sons, 1975.

Fulbright, Senator J. William. *The Arrogance of Power*. New York: Vintage Books, 1966.

Green, Mark J.; Fallows, James M.; and Zwick, David. *Who Runs Congress?* (Ralph Nader Congress Report). New York: Grossman, 1972.

Herzberg, D., and Peltason, J. W. *A Student Guide to Campaign Politics*. New York: McGraw-Hill, 1970.

Hess, Karl. *Dear America*. New York: William Morrow & Company, Inc., 1975.

How To Win Votes and Influence Elections. Chicago: Public Administration Service.

Irish, Marian D., and Prothro, James W. *The Politics of American Democracy*. 4th ed. Englewood Cliffs, N.J.: Prentice-Hall, 1968.

Jaquette, Jane S., ed. *Women In Politics*. New York: John Wiley and Sons, 1974.

Jewell, Malcolm E., and Patterson, Samuel, C. *The Legislative Process in the United States*. 2d ed. New York: Random House, 1966-1973.

Jones, W. Ron, with Cheever, Julia. *Finding Community*. Palo Alto, Cal.: James E. Freel and Associates, 1971.

Kaufman, Herbert. *Politics and Policies in State and Local Governments*. Englewood Cliffs, N.J.: Prentice-Hall, 1963.

Key, V. O., Jr. (completed with the assistance of Milton C. Cummings, Jr., after the 1960 death of Dr. Key). *The Responsible Electorate*. Cambridge: The Belknap Press of Harvard University Press, 1966.

Kofmehl, Kenneth. *Professional Staffs of Congress.* Lafayette, Ind.: Purdue University Press, 1962.

Lang, Curt, and Lang, Gladys Engel. *Politics and Television.* Chicago: Quadrangle Books, 1968.

Lieberman, Jethro K. *Understanding Our Constitution.* New York: Fawcett World Library, 1968.

Liston, Robert A. *Politics From Precinct to President.* New York: Delacorte Press, 1968.

————. *Your Career in Civil Service.* New York: Julian Messner, Inc., 1966.

Meyers, William, and Rinard, Park. *Making Activism Work.* New York: Gordon and Breach, Science Publishers, Inc., 1972.

Morrow, William L. *Congressional Committees.* New York: Charles Scribner's Sons, 1969.

Nader, Ralph, and Ross, Donald. *Action for a Change.* New York: Grossman, 1971.

Oberman, Joseph. *Planning and Managing the Economy of the City.* (Policy Guidelines for the Metropolitan Mayor). New York: Praeger Publishers, 1972.

Parkinson, Hank. *Winning Political Campaigns With Publicity.* Wichita, Kansas: Campaign Associates Press, 1973.

————. *Winning Your Campaign . . . A Nuts-and-Bolts Guide to Political Victory.* Englewood Cliffs, N.J.: Prentice-Hall, 1970.

Pezzuti, Thomas A. *You Can Fight City Hall & Win.* Los Angeles: Sherbourne Press, 1974.

Rapoport, Daniel. *Inside the House.* Chicago: Follett Publishing Co., 1975.

Redman, Eric. *The Dance of Legislation.* New York: Simon & Schuster, Inc., 1973.

Reilly, Thomas A., and Sigal, Michael W., eds. *New Patterns in American Politics.* New York: Praeger Publishers, 1975.

Riegle, Donald, with Armbrister, Trevor. *O Congress.* Garden City, N.Y.: Doubleday and Company, 1972.

Rogowski, Ronald. *Rational Legitimacy.* Princeton, N.J.: Princeton University Press, 1974.

Ross, Russell M., and Millsap, Kenneth F. *State and Local Government and Administration.* New York: The Ronald Press Company, 1966.

Salamanca, Lucy. *Fortress of Freedom—The Story of the Library of Congress.* Philadelphia: J. B. Lippincott Company, 1942.

Samish, Arthur, with Thomas, Bob. *The Secret Boss of California.* New York: Crown Publishers, 1971.

Stimson, Bullitt. *To Be a Politician—What it Means.* New York: Doubleday and Company, 1959.

Thompson, Dr. Hunter S. *Fear and Loathing on the Campaign Trail '72.* California: Straight Arrow Books, 1973.

de Tocqueville, Alexis. *Democracy in America.* New York: Vintage Books, 1959.

Tolchin, Susan, and Tolchin, Martin. *To the Victor.* New York: Random House, 1971.

Udall, Stewart L. *1976: Agenda for Tomorrow.* New York: Harcourt, Brace & World, Inc., 1968.

The Washington Lobby. 2nd ed. Congressional Quarterly, Washington, D.C., 1974.

The Washington Post, staff. "Bad Times and Beyond." With excerpts from selected position papers and transcripts of the White House "Economic Summit" of September, 1974.

Waterlow, Charlotte. *Superpowers and Victims.* Englewood Cliffs, N.J.: Prentice-Hall, 1974.

Weingast, David E. *We Elect a President.* New York: Julian Messner, Inc., 1973.

Wilson, Woodrow. *Congressional Government.* Originally published in 1885. New York: Meridian Books, 1956.

Wise, David. *The Politics of Lying.* New York: Random House, 1973.

Wright, Jim. *You and Your Congressman.* New York: Coward-McCann, Inc., 1965.

Zeigler, Harmon. *Interest Groups in American Society.* Englewood Cliffs, N.J.: Prentice-Hall, Inc., 1964.

Zinn, Dr. Charles J. *How Our Laws Are Made.* Superintendent of Documents. Washington, D.C.: Government Printing Office.

Campaign Associates, Inc., of Wichita, Kansas, specializes as political campaign consultants. The following bibliography has been compiled to answer the most frequent question asked by readers of their semimonthly periodical *Campaign Insight:* "What should I be reading?" Called "The Practical Politician's Library," the list is divided into categories for easy reference.

GENERAL

Atkins, Chester G., *et al. Getting Elected: A Guide to Winning State and Local Office.* Boston: Houghton, Mifflin, Co., 1973.

Banfield, Edward C., and Wilson, James Q. *City Politics.* New York: Vantage Books, 1974.

Barone, Michael, *et al. The Almanac of American Politics.* Boston: Gambit, 1972.

Baus, Herbert M., and Ross, Bill R. *Politics Battle Plan.* New York: Macmillan, 1974.

Boyarsky, Bill, and Boyarsky, Nancy. *Back Room Politics.* Los Angeles: J. P. Tarcher, 1974.

Coffman, Tom. *Catch a Wave.* Honolulu: The University of Hawaii Press, 1973.

Demaris, Ovid. *Dirty Business.* New York: Harper's Magazine Press, 1974.

Gilfond, Henry. *How to Run for School Office.* New York: Hawthorn Press, 1969.

Hershey, Marjory. *The Making of Campaign Strategy.* Lexington, Mass.: D. C. Heath Publishers, 1974.

Hoopes, Ray. *Getting With Politics.* New York: Darrell Publishing, 1969.

Huckshorn, Robert J., and Spencer, Robert C. *The Politics*

of *Defeat—Campaigning for Congress*. Amherst, Mass.: University of Massachusetts Press, 1970.

Irwin, W. P., and Michelon, L. C. *Understanding Politics*. Cleveland, Ohio: World Publishing, 1970.

Jekketm, Stanley, Jr. *Political Campaigning*. Washington, D.C.: Brookings Institute, 1970.

May, Ernest R., and Fraser, Janet. *Campaign Management —'72—The Managers Speak*. Cambridge, Mass.: Harvard University Press, 1973.

Merriam, Robert E. *Going Into Politics*. New York: Harper and Brothers, 1970.

Meyer, D. S. *The Winning Candidate*. New York: James H. Heineman, Inc., 1966.

Napolitan, Joseph. *The Election Game and How to Win It*. New York: Doubleday, 1972.

Rosenbloom, David, ed. *The Political Market Place*. New York: Quadrangle Books, 1972.

Schlesinger, Joseph. *Ambition and Politics*. Chicago: Rand McNally, 1966.

Schnier and Murphy. *Vote Power: The Official Activist Campaigner's Handbook*. New York: Doubleday, 1974.

Shadegg, Stephen. *The New How to Win An Election*. New York: Taplinger Publishing, 1972.

Simpson, Dick. *Winning Elections—A Handbook in Participatory Politics*. Chicago: Swallow Press, 1971.

Stone, William F. *The Psychology of Politics*. New York: The Free Press, 1974.

Theis, Paul A., and Steponkus, William P. *All About Politics*. Ann Arbor, Mich.: R. W. Bowker, 1972.

Tolchin, Susan, and Tolchin, Martin. *Clout! Womanpower and Politics*. New York: Coward, McCann & Geoghegan, Inc., 1973.

Torrance, Susan. *Grass Roots Government: The County in Politics*. Washington, D.C.: Luce Publishers, 1970.

Walzer, Michael. *Political Action—A Political Guide to Movement Politics*. New York: Quadrangle Books, 1971.

ELECTORATE/PARTIES

Binzen, Peter. *White Town, U.S.A.* New York: Vantage, 1971.

Bloom, Melvyn H. *Public Relations and Presidential Campaigns: A Crisis in Democracy.* New York: Thomas Y. Crowell Co., 1973.

Bowen, Don R. *Political Behavior of the American Public.* Columbus, Ohio: Charles E. Merrill Publishers, 1968.

Broder, David S. *The Party's Over.* New York: Harper and Row, 1972.

Davidson, Chambler. *Bi-Racial Politics.* Baton Rouge, La.: The Louisiana State University Press, 1972.

DeVries, Walter, and Tarrance, Lance. *The Ticket Splitter: A New Force in American Politics.* Grand Rapids, Mich.: William E. Erdmans Publishers, 1973.

Dutton, Frederick G. *Changing Sources of Power.* New York: McGraw-Hill, 1971.

Fishel, Jeff. *Party and Opposition.* New York: David McKay, 1973.

Hyman, Sidney. *Youth in Politics.* New York: Basic Books, 1972.

Janowitz, Morris. *Political Conflict.* New York: Quadrangle Books, 1970.

Kimball, Penn. *The Disconnected.* New York: Columbia University Press, 1972.

Lamb, Karl A. *As Orange Goes.* New York: W. W. Norton & Co., 1974.

Lane, Robert E. *Political Life.* New York: The Free Press, 1959.

Levy, Mark R., and Kramer, Michael S. *The Ethnic Factor— How America's Minorities Decide Elections.* New York: Simon & Schuster, Inc., 1973.

Lierson, Avery. *Politics and Parties.* New York: Alfred Knopf, 1970.

Lipset, Seymour Martin. *Political Man*. Garden City, N.Y.: Anchor Books, 1959.

Lubell, Samuel. *The Hidden Crisis in American Politics*. New York: W. W. Norton Co., 1970.

McKenna, George. *American Populism*. New York: G. P. Putnam's Sons, 1974.

Michels, Robert. *Political Parties*. New York: The Free Press, 1958.

Murphy, Hal, and Gulliver, Reg. *The Southern Strategy*. New York: Charles Scribner's Sons, 1971.

Newfield, Jack, and Greenfield, Jeff. *A Populist Manifesto: The Making of a New Majority*. New York: Praeger Publishers, 1972.

Nimmo, Dan. *Popular Images of Politics*. Englewood Cliffs, N.J.: Prentice-Hall, 1974.

Orum, Anthony. *The Seeds of Politics: Youth and Politics in America*. Englewood Cliffs, N.J.: Prentice-Hall, 1972.

Phillips, Kevin. *The Emerging Republican Majority*. New Rochelle, N.Y.: Arlington House, 1969.

Saloma, John S., and Sontag, Frederick H. *Parties*. New York: Alfred A. Knopf, 1974.

Scammon, Richard M., and Wattenberg, Ben J. *The Real Majority*. New York: Coward, McCann, 1970.

Stedman, Murray S., Jr. *Urban Politics*. Cambridge, Mass.: Winthrop Publishers, 1972.

Sunquist, James L. *Dynamics of the Party System*. Washington, D.C.: The Brookings Institute, 1973.

Voting and Registration in the Election of 1972. Series P-20, Number 352. Washington, D.C.: U. S. Government Printing Office, 1973, Oct.

Yankelovich, Daniel. *The Changing Values on Campus*. New York: Centum Square Press, 1972.

TECHNIQUES

Agranoff, Robert. *The New Style in Election Campaigns*. Boston: Holbrook Press, 1972.

Bruno, Jerry, and Greenfield, Jeff. *The Advance Man.* New York: William Morrow and Company, 1971.

Chartrand, Robert. *Computers and Political Campaigning.* New York: Spartan Books, 1974.

Evry, Hal. *The Selling of a Candidate—The Winning Formula.* Los Angeles: Western Opinion Research Center, 1970.

Hiebert, Ray *et al.*, eds. *The Political Image Merchants: Strategies and the New Politics.* Washington, D.C.: Acropolis Books, 1971.

Jonas, Frank H. *Political Dynamiting.* Salt Lake City, Utah: University of Utah Press, 1970.

Nimmo, Dan. *The Political Persuaders.* Englewood Cliffs, N.J.: Prentice-Hall, 1970.

Pohl, Frederick. *Practical Politics.* New York: Valentine Books, 1970.

Rosenbloom, David Lee. *The Election Men.* New York: Quadrangle Books, 1973.

Swartzman, Edward. *Campaign Craftsmanship.* New York: Universe Books, 1973.

Szostak, John, and Cottom, Mello. *Volunteer: The Lifeline of a Campaign.* (Private publication).

FUND RAISING

Alexander, Herbert. *Money in Politics.* Washington, D.C.: Public Affairs Press, 1974.

Archibald, Sam. *The Pollution of Politics.* Washington, D.C.: Public Affairs Press, 1974.

Domhoff, G. William. *Fat Cats and Democrats.* Englewood Cliffs, N.J.: Prentice-Hall, 1972.

Gilson, Lawrence. *Money and Secrecy.* New York: Praeger Publishers, 1972.

McCarthy, Max. *Elections For Sale.* Boston: Houghton, Mifflin Company, 1972.

Smith, Judith G., ed. *Political Brokers*. New York: Liveright, 1972.

Thayer, George. *Who Shakes the Money Tree?* New York: Simon & Schuster, Inc., 1974.

Tips on Political Fund Raising . . . With Side Trips Into Budgeting and Legal Aspects. Staff written. Wichita, Kansas: Campaign Associates Press, 1974.

PUBLICITY / PRESS

Crouse, Timothy. *The Boys on the Bus*. New York: Ballantine Books, 1973.

ADVERTISING

Fochs, Arnold. *Advertising That Won Elections*. Duluth, Minn.: A. J. Publishing, 1974.

Lang, Kurt, and Lang, Gladys E. *Politics and Television*. New York: Quadrangle, 1968.

McGinnis, Joe. *The Selling of the President, 1968*. New York: Trident Press, 1969.

Mickelson, Sid. *Television*. New York: Dodd, Mead and Company, 1970.

Minow, Newton N., *et al. Presidential Television*. New York: Basic Books, 1973.

POLLING / SURVEY

Bean, Louis H. *The Art of Forecasting*. New York: Random House, 1975.

Bogart, Leo. *Silent Politics: Polls and the Awareness of Public Opinion*. New York: Wiley-Interscience Publishers, 1972.

Bongean, Nemo. *Political Attitudes and Public Opinion*. New York: David McKay, 1972.

Roll, Charles W., and Cantril, Albert H. *Polls: Their Use and Misuse in Politics*. New York: Basic Books, 1972.

Periodicals are a constant and current reference source. For balanced comment and information, it is best to read several of the top rated major newspapers and reference magazines listed below in alphabetical order.

The American Political Science Review
Boston Globe
Business Week
Chicago Tribune
Christian Science Monitor
Congressional Quarterly Weekly Reports
Fortune
Los Angeles Times
Louisville Courier-Journal
Miami Herald
Milwaukee Journal
The Nation
The National Review
The New Republic
Newsday
Newsweek
New York Times
PS—The American Political Science Association Quarterly
The Sacramento Bee
Scientific American
Time
U. S. News and World Report
Wall Street Journal
Washington Post
Vista (United Nations Magazine)

Copies of the above periodicals can be found in most local community and college libraries. Back issues are usually preserved on film.

INDEX

ABOUT THE AUTHOR

A nationally known interior designer, Robert V. Doyle phased out a lifetime career of more than thirty-five years in that profession, and turned in retirement to two of his hobbies—writing and photography.

With a peripheral interest in the political scene since his youth in then-socialist Milwaukee, Wisconsin, Mr. Doyle has been involved in California Democratic campaigns. He has also been a precinct election officer. It is interesting that he would become a free-lance feature writer for the *California Republican*. This assignment mandated in-depth research in elective government and the many facets of the policymaking arena. Now a contributor to *Campaign Insight*, Mr. Doyle is concentrating on government and politics in future literary projects. His home-office is only three freeway-minutes from the Sacramento capitol complex, where he and Mrs. Doyle spend much time researching and interviewing political personalities.

In his second career, Mr. Doyle has also written national magazine articles about Alaskan big-game hunting, camping, elementary education, golf, home decorating, marketing, retailing, and careers for young people.